Joyce Appleby on *Thomas Jefferson*
Louis Auchincloss on *Theodore Roosevelt*
Jean H. Baker on *James Buchanan*
H. W. Brands on *Woodrow Wilson*
Alan Brinkley on *John F. Kennedy*
Douglas Brinkley on *Gerald R. Ford*
Josiah Bunting III on *Ulysses S. Grant*
James MacGregor Burns and Susan Dunn on *George Washington*
Charles W. Calhoun on *Benjamin Harrison*
Gail Collins on *William Henry Harrison*
Robert Dallek on *Harry S. Truman*
John W. Dean on *Warren G. Harding*
John Patrick Diggins on *John Adams*
Elizabeth Drew on *Richard M. Nixon*
John S. D. Eisenhower on *Zachary Taylor*
Paul Finkelman on *Millard Fillmore*
Annette Gordon-Reed on *Andrew Johnson*
Henry F. Graff on *Grover Cleveland*
David Greenberg on *Calvin Coolidge*
Gary Hart on *James Monroe*
Michael F. Holt on *Franklin Pierce*
Roy Jenkins on *Franklin Delano Roosevelt*
Zachary Karabell on *Chester Alan Arthur*
Lewis H. Lapham on *William Howard Taft*
William E. Leuchtenburg on *Herbert Hoover*
Gary May on *John Tyler*
George McGovern on *Abraham Lincoln*
Timothy Naftali on *George H. W. Bush*
Charles Peters on *Lyndon B. Johnson*
Kevin Phillips on *William McKinley*
Robert V. Remini on *John Quincy Adams*
Ira Rutkow on *James A. Garfield*
John Seigenthaler on *James K. Polk*
Hans L. Trefousse on *Rutherford B. Hayes*
Tom Wicker on *Dwight D. Eisenhower*
Ted Widmer on *Martin Van Buren*
Sean Wilentz on *Andrew Jackson*
Garry Wills on *James Madison*
Julian E. Zelizer on *Jimmy Carter*

ALSO BY MICHAEL F. HOLT

By One Vote: The Disputed Presidential Election of 1876

The Fate of Their Country:
Politicians, Slavery Extension, and the Coming of the Civil War

The Civil War and Reconstruction, 3rd edition
(with Jean Harvey Baker and David Herbert Donald)

The Rise and Fall of the American Whig Party:
Jacksonian Politics and the Onset of the Civil War

Political Parties and American Political Development from
the Age of Jackson to the Age of Lincoln

A Master's Due: Essays in Honor of David Herbert Donald
(ed. with William J. Cooper, Jr., and John McCardell)

The Political Crisis of the 1850s

Forging a Majority: The Formation of the
Republican Party in Pittsburgh, 1848–1860

Franklin Pierce

Michael F. Holt

Franklin
Pierce

THE AMERICAN PRESIDENTS

ARTHUR M. SCHLESINGER, JR., AND SEAN WILENTZ

GENERAL EDITORS

Times Books

HENRY HOLT AND COMPANY, NEW YORK

Times Books
Henry Holt and Company, LLC
Publishers since 1866
175 Fifth Avenue
New York, New York 10010
www.henryholt.com

Henry Holt® is a registered trademark of Henry Holt and Company, LLC.

Library of Congress Cataloging-in-Publication Data
Holt, Michael F. (Michael Fitzgibbon)
    Franklin Pierce / Michael F. Holt.—1st ed.
        p. cm.—(The American presidents series)
    Includes bibliographical references and index.
    ISBN 978-0-8050-8719-2
    1. Pierce, Franklin, 1804–1869.   2. Presidents—United States—Biography.
3. United States—Politics and government—1853–1857.   I. Title.
    E432.H65 2010
    973.6'6092–dc22
    [B]   2009036425

Henry Holt books are available for special promotions and
premiums. For details contact: Director, Special Markets.

First Edition 2010

Printed in the United States of America
1   3   5   7   9   10   8   6   4   2

For my grandson,
Fox Fitzgibbon Sloane

Contents

Editor's Note

THE AMERICAN PRESIDENCY

The president is the central player in the American political order. That would seem to contradict the intentions of the Founding Fathers. Remembering the horrid example of the British monarchy, they invented a separation of powers in order, as Justice Brandeis later put it, "to preclude the exercise of arbitrary power." Accordingly, they divided the government into three allegedly equal and coordinate branches—the executive, the legislative, and the judiciary.

But a system based on the tripartite separation of powers has an inherent tendency toward inertia and stalemate. One of the three branches must take the initiative if the system is to move. The executive branch alone is structurally capable of taking that initiative. The Founders must have sensed this when they accepted Alexander Hamilton's proposition in the Seventieth Federalist that "energy in the executive is a leading character in the definition of good government." They thus envisaged a strong president—but within an equally strong system of constitutional accountability. (The term *imperial presidency* arose in the 1970s to describe the situation when the balance between power and accountability is upset in favor of the executive.)

The American system of self-government thus comes to focus in the presidency—"the vital place of action in the system," as Woodrow Wilson put it. Henry Adams, himself the great-grandson and grandson of presidents as well as the most brilliant of American historians, said that the American president "resembles the commander of a ship at sea. He must have a helm to grasp, a course to steer, a port to seek." The men in the White House (thus far only men, alas) in steering their chosen courses have shaped our destiny as a nation.

Biography offers an easy education in American history, rendering the past more human, more vivid, more intimate, more accessible, more connected to ourselves. Biography reminds us that presidents are not supermen. They are human beings too, worrying about decisions, attending to wives and children, juggling balls in the air, and putting on their pants one leg at a time. Indeed, as Emerson contended, "There is properly no history; only biography."

Presidents serve us as inspirations, and they also serve us as warnings. They provide bad examples as well as good. The nation, the Supreme Court has said, has "no right to expect that it will always have wise and humane rulers, sincerely attached to the principles of the Constitution. Wicked men, ambitious of power, with hatred of liberty and contempt of law, may fill the place once occupied by Washington and Lincoln."

The men in the White House express the ideals and the values, the frailties and the flaws, of the voters who send them there. It is altogether natural that we should want to know more about the virtues and the vices of the fellows we have elected to govern us. As we know more about them, we will know more about ourselves. The French political philosopher Joseph de Maistre said, "Every nation has the government it deserves."

At the start of the twenty-first century, forty-two men have made it to the Oval Office. (George W. Bush is counted our forty-third president, because Grover Cleveland, who served nonconsecutive terms, is counted twice.) Of the parade of presidents, a dozen or so lead the polls periodically conducted by historians and political scientists. What makes a great president?

Great presidents possess, or are possessed by, a vision of an ideal America. Their passion, as they grasp the helm, is to set the ship of state on the right course toward the port they seek. Great presidents also have a deep psychic connection with the needs, anxieties, dreams of people. "I do not believe," said Wilson, "that any man can lead who does not act . . . under the impulse of a profound sympathy with those whom he leads—a sympathy which is insight—an insight which is of the heart rather than of the intellect."

"All of our great presidents," said Franklin D. Roosevelt, "were leaders of thought at a time when certain ideas in the life of the nation had to be clarified." So Washington incarnated the idea of federal union, Jefferson and Jackson the idea of democracy, Lincoln union and freedom, Cleveland rugged honesty. Theodore Roosevelt and Wilson, said FDR, were both "moral leaders, each in his own way and his own time, who used the presidency as a pulpit."

To succeed, presidents not only must have a port to seek but they must convince Congress and the electorate that it is a port worth seeking. Politics in a democracy is ultimately an educational process, an adventure in persuasion and consent. Every president stands in Theodore Roosevelt's bully pulpit.

The greatest presidents in the scholars' rankings, Washington, Lincoln, and Franklin Roosevelt, were leaders who confronted and overcame the republic's greatest crises. Crisis widens presidential opportunities for bold and imaginative action. But it does not guarantee presidential greatness. The crisis of secession did not spur Buchanan or the crisis of depression spur Hoover to creative leadership. Their inadequacies in the face of crisis allowed Lincoln and the second Roosevelt to show the difference individuals make to history. Still, even in the absence of first-order crisis, forceful and persuasive presidents—Jefferson, Jackson, James K. Polk, Theodore Roosevelt, Harry Truman, John F. Kennedy, Ronald Reagan, George W. Bush—are able to impose their own priorities on the country.

The diverse drama of the presidency offers a fascinating set of tales. Biographies of American presidents constitute a chronicle of wisdom and folly, nobility and pettiness, courage and cunning, forthrightness and deceit, quarrel and consensus. The turmoil perennially swirling around the White House illuminates the heart of the American democracy.

It is the aim of the American Presidents series to present the grand panorama of our chief executives in volumes compact enough for the busy reader, lucid enough for the student, authoritative enough for the scholar. Each volume offers a distillation of character and career. I hope that these lives will give readers some understanding of the pitfalls and potentialities of the presidency and also of the responsibilities of citizenship. Truman's famous sign—"The buck stops here"—tells only half the story. Citizens cannot escape the ultimate responsibility. It is in the voting booth, not on the presidential desk, that the buck finally stops.

—Arthur M. Schlesinger, Jr.

Franklin Pierce

Preface

Franklin Pierce was arguably the most handsome man ever to serve as president of the United States. He was certainly one of the most amiable and congenial men to hold that office. Because of his popularity, personal charm, and family lineage, he enjoyed a meteoric political career in New Hampshire. Still in his twenties, he was elected four consecutive years to the state house of representatives, and in the final two of those terms his admiring colleagues chose him as Speaker. New Hampshire's voters sent him to the national House of Representatives in 1833 and again in 1835, and in 1837, prior to his thirty-third birthday, the state legislature put him in the U.S. Senate, from which he resigned in early 1842. As a brigadier general commanding volunteer regiments raised in New England, he earned a commendable, if not quite glorious, record in the Mexican-American War. Democrats nominated him for president in 1852 in order to break a deadlock at their national convention, and in November, a few days before his forty-eighth birthday, he carried twenty-seven of thirty-one states to become the youngest man yet elected to the White House.

Pierce's career had been marred by personal tragedy. Two of

his sons had died before reaching the age of five, and shortly before he left New Hampshire for his inauguration in Washington, D.C., the last of his young sons was killed in a train accident. His painfully shy and often morose wife, who hated politics and life in Washington, grew to be more a source of concern than of solace.

During his term in the White House, Pierce could have used a helpmeet. Historians, indeed, usually rank Pierce among the six or eight worst presidents the country has ever had. Two things primarily account for that negative judgment. A passionately committed Democratic Party loyalist, Pierce during his presidency managed to divide his party into fiercely warring factional camps. More important, he helped propel the nation down the road to the Civil War. As a result, Democrats suffered monumental defeats in the off-year congressional elections of 1854–55 and were reduced to a minority of the national electorate, a status they would suffer until the mid-1870s. Also as a result, Pierce was the only president in the nineteenth century who sought, but was denied, renomination by his beloved party.

Various explanations have been offered for this sorry record. Some attribute it to personal mistakes in judgment and a lack of farsighted statesmanship on Pierce's part. Others portray Pierce, for all his amiability, as a fundamentally weak man who craved the approval of his peers and who deferred to stronger personalities in his cabinet and party. Still others cite external forces over which he had no control and which overwhelmed his presidency. As I hope to show in the following brief biography, all three factors played a role in wrecking what had once been a dazzlingly successful political career.

I argue here, however, that the primary factor bringing

Pierce to grief was his obsession with preserving the unity of the Democratic Party. Almost every previous biographer and historian who has studied Pierce has noted that deep commitment, but none has successfully explained what caused it. I contend that it derived from Pierce's understanding of the political situation in which he usually found himself, namely the lopsided dominance of his own Democratic Party vis-à-vis its partisan foes. Starting in the 1820s, newspaper editors affiliated with New York's Martin Van Buren astutely outlined the danger to any party's internal cohesion that a weak external opposition poses. Any party may "suffer temporary defeats," those editors wrote, but "it is certain to acquire additional strength by the attacks of adverse parties." A party is "most in jeopardy when an opposition is not sufficiently defined." Or again, during the contest between Jeffersonians and Federalists, "each found in the strength of the other a powerful motive of union and vigor." In sum, the internal unity of any party depends on the robustness, the closeness, of interparty competition. The weaker that external competition, the greater is the danger of internal fragmentation within the dominant party.

Pierce was an undergraduate at Bowdoin College in Maine when these newspaper editorials appeared in Albany, New York, and I have no evidence that he read them. Nonetheless, a private letter Pierce wrote to a friend in the mid-1820s about the necessity of political parties and interparty competition in any republic suggests that in fact he did. In any event, he acted throughout his political career as though he had read them. His Democratic Party was overwhelmingly dominant in New Hampshire from the early 1830s until the early 1850s and in the nation as a whole, if only temporarily, from the fall of 1851 until the fall of 1854. That dominance, and the threat it posed to internal Democratic unity, primarily, if not exclusively, accounts for Franklin Pierce's most fateful political decisions as the country faced the ever-growing prospect of civil war.

In closing I want to thank Robin Dennis and Sean Wilentz for their editorial help in preparing this book.

1

A Precocious Start

Franklin Pierce was born on November 23, 1804, in Hillsborough, New Hampshire. He was the sixth child of Anna Kendrick Pierce and General Benjamin Pierce, who also had a daughter from a previous marriage. Pierce later described his mother as affectionate and endlessly forgiving of his youthful hijinks, but it was his far sterner father, the most influential man in Hillsborough County, who had the greater impact on him. A native of Chelmsford, Massachusetts, Benjamin Pierce had enlisted in the Continental army as a teenager as soon as he heard about the fighting at Lexington and Concord. He fought in the battles of Breed's Hill and Ticonderoga, among others, and spent the winter with George Washington at Valley Forge. He was mustered out of the army with a medal from Washington, and at the rank of lieutenant, in 1784. In short, he had the credentials of a Revolutionary War hero, and his war stories inspired young Franklin with a desire to emulate his father's military service. That two of his older brothers as well as his half sister's husband fought in the War of 1812 intensified this yen.

His reputation as a war hero served Benjamin Pierce well

when he moved to the frontier town of Hillsborough in western New Hampshire in 1786. Not only would he quickly become the commanding general of the state's militia, but he was also elected to several terms as the county's sheriff, where he became famous for his generosity toward jailed debtors. He also sat on the governor's council. In the late 1820s, he served two one-year terms as governor of the state. Benjamin Pierce was a Jeffersonian Republican who loathed Federalists as elitist snobs, and that hatred deepened when a Federalist majority in the state legislature purged him from the office of sheriff after he had defied an order from a Federalist judge.

Frank Pierce was hardly a bookish youth. He loved the outdoors and enjoyed roughhousing, swimming, fishing, and ice skating far more than lessons in school. Even as a boy he evinced the personal charm that would smooth his political rise. He was his playmates' ringleader, and adults, especially adult women, found him an altogether winning lad—honest, polite, and poised. To put it differently—and perhaps more ominously—from boyhood on Pierce was eager to please other people. Pierce did not like school, but his father, who lacked a formal education of his own, was determined that his sons attend college. Thus Pierce was dispatched to a series of academies outside Hillsborough to learn Latin and Greek in preparation for the required college entrance exams. One of Pierce's older brothers had attended West Point and another Dartmouth College. When the time came to send Frank off to college, however, Federalists controlled Dartmouth, and Benjamin Pierce would not consider it. He determined instead to send Frank to Bowdoin College in Brunswick, Maine.

Pierce and his parents arrived in Brunswick for the beginning of the 1820 fall term several months before Frank's sixteenth birthday. Bowdoin was then a very small college, but it attracted an astonishing number of young men destined for national eminence. William Pitt Fessenden, the future Whig and Republican U.S. senator from Maine, was in the class ahead of Pierce's, and James Bradbury, a future Democratic senator from Maine, was in the student body at the same time. John P. Hale, who would later run against Pierce for president, was a freshman when Pierce was a senior. Calvin Stowe, the future husband of Harriet Beecher Stowe, was valedictorian of Pierce's class. Henry Wadsworth Longfellow was in the class of 1825, and two other members of that class would play important roles in Pierce's future life. One was Jonathan Cilley of New Hampshire, later a Democratic congressman who lived in the same boardinghouse with Pierce in Washington during one of his congressional terms. The other was Nathaniel Hawthorne, who remained Pierce's lifelong friend and who would write a campaign biography for him in 1852.

While he struggled with mathematics, Pierce's training in classical languages served him well—indeed too well—during his first years at Bowdoin. The cold fact is that during his first two years, Pierce played far more than he studied. He frequently skipped mandatory recitation periods in order to hike in the nearby woods or fish in nearby streams. In the dormitory at night, when solitary study was the prescribed regimen, Pierce was famous for bursting into other students' rooms to start furniture-smashing wrestling matches. He usually won those contests. Ten years later, a fellow Democratic state legislator with whom Pierce tussled described him as "the most powerful man of his size I know of." Wrestling was not Pierce's only nighttime activity in those first years at Bowdoin. In violation of the school's rules, Pierce and his closest pals snuck out of the dorm to frequent a Brunswick tavern.

Heavy drinking and Pierce's name go together like a horse and carriage, and years later his political opponents would label him a drunkard. In the 1820s, young men were as likely as those today to seek amusement and drink heavily in bars, and there seems little doubt that the gregarious and fun-loving Pierce enjoyed socializing with his friends. From his perspective, not to do so would be an insult to those friends. It appears that his tolerance for alcoholic intake was low and that he often became riotously giddy much sooner than his drinking partners. But there is no evidence that Pierce's drinking sprees impaired his mental faculties once he had sobered up. Some of Pierce's behavior then and especially after he left the White House suggests that he suffered from alcoholism, but at this distance in time it is impossible to render a definitive diagnosis.

As a result of Pierce's carefree behavior, he ranked dead last academically in his class by the end of his sophomore year at Bowdoin. When he learned of his embarrassing status, he determined to reform. Gone were the hikes in the woods and the evenings in the tavern. Instead of copying other students' work to turn in as his own as he had done for two years, he arose at 4 A.M. every morning to hit the books. Overseeing this transformation to academic self-discipline was a new member of his class, a devout Methodist from Maine named Zenas Caldwell, who brought Pierce home with him during the midwinter break. In his senior year, Pierce roomed with the sober-minded Caldwell, and with the help of his strict supervision the one-time dunce graduated fifth in his class, now reduced to fourteen students, and had the honor of delivering a seven-minute disquisition in Latin at graduation in August 1824.

Pierce was far too fun-loving and far too addicted to outdoor exercise, however, to become a total bookworm. In the spring of his junior year he organized a military company called the Bowdoin Cadets, which "Captain" Pierce led in marching drills around the campus. Like most colleges in that day, Bowdoin boasted rival debating societies, and during Pierce's senior year, the impending presidential election of 1824 became the focus of their competition. One of these societies proclaimed the merits of John Quincy Adams, while, tellingly, Pierce's club touted those of Andrew Jackson.

After graduation Pierce returned to his parents' house in Hillsborough and began to read law with a local attorney. He moved to Portsmouth, New Hampshire, in the spring of 1825 to study in the office of Levi Woodbury and, after Woodbury left to serve in the U.S. Senate, to another lawyer in Northampton, Massachusetts. He completed his legal studies in Amherst, New Hampshire, the Hillsborough county seat, and was admitted to the bar there in September 1827, two months shy of his twenty-third birthday. He then returned to Hillsborough to start his practice.

The interest Pierce developed in national politics at Bowdoin quickened during his months in Portsmouth, a former Federalist and now pro-Adams bastion. Like other supporters of Andrew Jackson, Pierce was infuriated by the so-called Corrupt Bargain that had placed Adams in the White House. He sympathized with the efforts of Woodbury and Isaac Hill, a Concord editor, to organize a pro-Jackson opposition party. "A Republic without parties is a complete anomaly," he wrote a friend. "The citizens are convinced that Jeffersonian principles are the principles for a free people, and I trust they have no notion of renouncing their faith."

Pierce put these beliefs into practice when he returned to Hillsborough. In 1827 his father was elected governor for the first time with no organized opposition, but in 1828, the presidential election year, pro-Adams men rallied to stop his reelection. Frank Pierce campaigned aggressively for his father. He helped organize a pro-Jackson demonstration on the anniversary of Jackson's victory at the Battle of New Orleans in January. Two months later, Frank made his formal political debut at the annual Hillsborough town meeting. Town meetings in

New Hampshire did more than discuss local affairs. They also cast votes each year for state officials and, in odd years, for U.S. congressmen. Hillsborough, like many other New Hampshire towns, was divided between Adams and Jackson men. To the surprise of many, Jacksonians elected young Frank Pierce moderator of the meeting, as they would during the next five successive years. That, however, was the only Pierce victory that March. Benjamin's bid for reelection failed, an accurate portent of Jackson's defeat in New Hampshire in the presidential election the following November. Yet Benjamin, now openly aligned with the Jacksonians, would win the governorship again in March 1829, and at the Hillsborough town meeting that year Franklin Pierce, barely twenty-four years old, was unanimously elected to the state legislature. The town meeting repeated that choice over the next three years, and in the final two of them Pierce's admiring colleagues in the state house of representatives elected him their Speaker.

• • •

Pierce's interest in politics, devotion to Jeffersonian principles, and deep commitment to the new Jacksonian Democratic Party endured for the remainder of his life. Nonetheless, he had studied law to earn a living, not to run for office. Initially his practice was confined primarily to the semiannual sessions of the county court of common pleas in Amherst. He lost his first case there in the spring of 1828, but gradually he developed into a very successful advocate. Pierce lacked an incisive legal mind, but he had other attributes that served him well in the civil and criminal cases he argued before juries. He displayed a prodigious memory for names and faces, a trait that obviously benefited him in his political career as well. He could address individual jurors by name when pleading cases, and he would remember those names for years thereafter. He had a deep, rich voice, again a trait that helped his political career because his audience could actually hear his unamplified voice at political rallies. Most important, he exuded a personal charm, an amiable temperament, and an instinctive human empathy. Pierce directed his arguments to the emotions of jurors, not to their collective logic, and he usually won.

The state legislature met in Concord each June, between the semiannual sessions of the court of common pleas, and occasionally in November and December, after the fall session. Much of the legislature's business was so humdrum that no one even bothered to demand roll-call votes. The public policy issues that evoked partisan conflict between the Adams men, who referred to themselves as National Republicans after Adams's defeat by Jackson in 1828, and the fledgling Jacksonians were primarily economic: the role of government in constructing internal improvements such as turnpikes, canals, and railroads; the incorporation of, and the privileges awarded to shareholders in, corporations, especially those that absolved them from any responsibility for companies' debts; and banking and paper money. Indeed, most partisan conflict between 1834 and 1856, what historians call the Second American Party System, was fueled by these issues.

In New Hampshire, these questions, especially those surrounding the chartering of banks and railroad companies, had a regional dimension. The coastal towns of southeastern New Hampshire were the first settled in the state, had once been Federalist strongholds, and were closely aligned with business interests in Boston. They had financial stakes in locating banks in and pushing railroad tracks to the more recently settled western and northern regions of the state. Many residents of those western and northern areas, in turn, viewed Boston-owned banks and especially Boston-owned railroads as outside imperial monopolists that would gut farming folk for their own distant profit. The legislative tussles over these issues catalyzed Franklin Pierce's commitment to what would soon develop into Jacksonian orthodoxy: opposition to any government subsidization of economic development, to corporate privilege, and to paper-money banking.

Beyond the reinforcement of these rigid policy stances, however, something more important was happening in New Hampshire between 1829 and 1832. Benjamin Pierce's reelection as governor as an avowed Jackson man in 1829 heralded New Hampshire's transition from a competitive state to a granite-ribbed Democratic one. In 1832, when his primary opponent was the Kentuckian Henry Clay, rather than the New Englander Adams, Andrew Jackson would carry New Hampshire, and from that date until the mid-1850s New Hampshire would remain the most reliably Democratic state in the North. During Pierce's four brief terms in the state legislature, New Hampshire became the political anomaly of New England, certainly an anomaly compared to its neighbors to the south and west. Not only would Massachusetts and Vermont become veritable fortresses of Whiggery, but both, especially Vermont, were swept by the Antimasonic tornado in the late 1820s and early 1830s. From 1831 to 1837, indeed, Antimasons won every annual gubernatorial election in Vermont, and it was the only state carried by the Antimasonic candidate for president in 1832. By contrast, Antimasons had negligible sway in New Hampshire, although they did manage to run a separate congressional ticket in 1833 that helped divide those who opposed the dominant Democrats.

One of the most important—if also most mystifying—political phenomena of the 1820s and 1830s, the Antimasonic Party represented a populistic grassroots protest movement against the purported legal, economic, social, and political privileges of members of Masonic lodges vis-à-vis nonmembers or outsiders. Its political goals were to purge Masons from elective and appointive public offices and then to eradicate Masonry altogether by stripping Masonic lodges of their state charters and making membership in the fraternity a criminal offense. Confined primarily to northeastern states, it attracted those who harbored grievances against the dominant party or faction of each particular state, whether it was the friends of Adams in Vermont and Massachusetts or those of Andrew Jackson in New York and Pennsylvania.

Because the economies, topography, and mix of religious denominations were so similar in Vermont and neighboring New Hampshire, historians have long been puzzled about why Antimasons were so strong in the former and so weak in the latter. One answer may be the stark difference in the competitive balance between Adams men (i.e., National Republicans) and Jacksonians in the two states. In 1828 Adams won 75 percent of Vermont's popular vote compared to Jackson's meager 25 percent. In New Hampshire, in contrast, Adams edged Jackson 52 percent to 48 percent. For those opposed to National Republicans who controlled both states, a new party may have seemed far more necessary in lopsided Vermont than in closely contested New Hampshire.

Franklin Pierce benefited markedly from New Hampshire's unique political trajectory. Because the 250 members of the state legislature assembled in Concord in June, rival state parties held their state conventions there that month so that members of the legislature could represent their home districts. Until the mid-1840s, New Hampshire chose its congressmen on statewide general tickets, rather than by individual districts. And in June 1832, the Democratic state convention put Pierce, then only twenty-seven years old, on the Democratic slate of five congressional candidates to be chosen by town meetings the following March. By 1832 that nomination virtually guaranteed his election; he went on to receive almost 76 percent of the statewide vote. His political horizons had widened.

A New Hampshire newspaper editorial at the time of his nomination merits quotation, for it identifies this fun-loving, friendly, and politically talented young man as the state's emerging favorite son. "Frank Pierce is the most popular man of his age that I know of in N.H.—praises in every one's mouth. Every circumstance connected with him seems to contribute to his popularity. In the first place, he has the advantage of his father's well earned reputation to bring him forward, and there is aristocracy enough, even in a community democratic as our own, to make this of no trifling importance to a young man just starting his life. In the next place he has a handsome person, bland and agreeable manners, a prompt and off-hand manner of saying and doing things, and talents competent to sustain himself in any station." As would become clear later in Pierce's political career, that last encomium was mistaken.

• • •

Between his election in March and the meeting of the Twenty-third Congress in December, Pierce had the thrill of meeting his hero Jackson as well as Vice President Martin Van Buren when they came to Concord during a summer tour of New England. The experience made Pierce an even firmer supporter of the administration when he reached Washington. Once there, he found lodging with a group of senators: Isaac Hill, whom the New Hampshire legislature had sent to the Senate, and his wife; both of Maine's senators; Senator William Wilkins of Pennsylvania; and Senator Hugh Lawson White of Tennessee. Pierce's closest friend in this Capitol Hill "mess," however, was Benjamin B. French, a former colleague in the New Hampshire legislature who had come to Washington to take a clerkship in the House of Representatives and who had brought his vivacious wife with him. Throughout Pierce's nine years in Congress, French would remain his closest confidant in the capital city.

Jackson's removal of federal deposits from the Bank of the United States by executive fiat in the fall of 1833 set the main agenda for this congressional session. Among other things, Jackson's alleged executive usurpation caused various opponents of that action in the Senate—National Republicans, South Carolina Nullifiers, who still maintained that a single state could void a federal law within its borders, and southerners who dubbed themselves Independent States Rights men—to coalesce as the new Whig Party. During the summer and fall of 1834, Antimasons in most of the northern states would join this new anti-Jackson party, and the coalition would take control of the Senate. The Whig Senate passed bills and resolutions commanding Jackson to restore the deposits to the Bank of the United States, but each time such bills reached the House, Jacksonians, including Pierce, easily defeated them. Pierce became a staunch Democrat, voting against every internal improvements bill that came up and against a measure giving preemption rights to squatters on federal lands in the West. Most of his time, however, was occupied by off-stage and often routine work for the judiciary committee, although he did manage to give one speech during the session on Revolutionary War pensions. To his great pleasure, this speech won him congratulations from a number of southern members of the House. For the remainder of his political career, Pierce would seek similar southern approval.

Between the first and second sessions of Congress, Pierce was married to Jane Means Appleton of Amherst, to whom he had become officially engaged in January 1833. Pierce first met Jane when he studied law in Amherst during 1827, but it's not clear how long he courted her before their engagement. They seemed an unlikely pair. For one thing, her family was wealthy and Federalist. One of her aunts, indeed, had married the Federalist senator Jeremiah Mason, while another was married to Amos Lawrence, the fabulously rich Boston textile manufacturer. Jacksonian Democrats they were not. For another, with dark auburn hair, blue eyes, a square jaw, and a slender, muscular physique, Franklin Pierce was a strikingly handsome man. The dark-haired Jane was no beauty. They also had quite different personalities. Pierce was gregarious, a paragon of health who loved out-of-doors physical activity. Jane was painfully shy, relentlessly prim, physically frail and sickly, and given to frequent bouts of melancholy. She loathed any use of tobacco or alcohol, and she soon grew to loathe politics and public life just as deeply. Surrounded by servants, she had no experience keeping house and was thoroughly daunted by the prospect. What they saw in each other is unclear. But opposites can attract, and on November 19, 1834, they married in her grandmother's mansion in Amherst, where she had been living for years. Portentously, within half an hour of exchanging vows, the couple left for Washington and the new session of Congress. Jane's poor health prevented much socializing by the newlyweds, and during these few months Frank abstained from drinking.

At the Democratic state convention in June 1834, Pierce was renominated for Congress, and in March 1835 he led the at-large Democratic slate to victory with 63 percent of the vote against the Whig ticket. Jane was pregnant and did not accompany Pierce to Washington for the opening of the Twenty-fourth Congress. She spent most of the winter and spring in Amherst with her mother and grandmother. So once again, Pierce made his quarters in a "mess," this time headed by the Democratic titan Senator Thomas Hart Benton of Missouri, whom Pierce quickly befriended.

The first session of the Twenty-fourth Congress proved more consequential for, and more revealing about, Franklin Pierce than any other term he served in Congress. From December 1835 until the session's close, much of his time was devoted to behind-the-scenes work on the judiciary committee and a special select committee to investigate the rechartering of banks in the District of Columbia. But the issue that preoccupied this legislative session, and especially the House's deliberations, was how to handle the thousands of petitions pouring into Washington demanding that Congress abolish slavery in the district. That issue led to a very public clash between Pierce and Senator John C. Calhoun of South Carolina.

Pierce was hardly proslavery, but he detested the abolitionist movement almost from the moment that it began to organize in the early 1830s. Never a particularly religious or pious man, quite unlike his new wife, he found the holier-than-thou attitude of abolitionists, and their penchant for condemning anyone who did not join their movement as a sinner, deeply offensive, indeed intolerable. Equally important, he feared that abolitionist agitation, if unchecked, could rend the nation his revered father had fought to create. Pierce was committed to the preservation of the Union, and he resented and rejected anything that he believed might threaten its perpetuity. Over time, Pierce's instant hatred of abolitionists evolved into hostility to any northern group that opposed slavery and its expansion westward in any way, even if it did not seek immediate abolition. By the 1850s, moreover, his stance on sectional disputes over slavery and its western expansion was flatly prosouthern, not simply anti-antislavery.

The abolitionist question came to a head early in December 1835, when Representative James H. Hammond of South Carolina demanded that the House summarily reject abolitionist petitions without considering or even officially receiving them.

For Pierce and many other congressmen, including some south-erners, this was too much, for it violated the people's constitu-tionally guaranteed right of petition. The proper course, Pierce told the House in a speech on December 18, was to receive but then automatically table such petitions without any further consideration, the solution that the House would ultimately adopt in May 1836 in what became known as the Gag Rule. But in his December 1835 speech, Pierce went further. Aboli-tionists were a tiny minority of fanatics, he declared; southern-ers should not identify them as representative of northern public opinion. In New Hampshire, he boasted, there was "not one in a hundred who does not entertain the most sacred regard for the rights of their Southern brethren—nay not one in five hundred who would not have those rights protected at any and every hazard."

In the first week of February 1836, tragedy struck. Pierce learned that Jane had given birth to a son and had survived the trials of labor, news that thrilled and relieved him. But joy quickly turned to grief when a subsequent letter reported that the boy had died three days later. Meanwhile, the work of Con-gress went on. On February 8 the House had appointed a select committee, chaired by South Carolinian Henry L. Pinckney, to consider proposals for handling abolitionist petitions. Pierce was named to the committee. When the Senate turned to the petition question on February 12, Calhoun, who was appar-ently trying to awaken his fellow southerners to the danger posed by abolitionists, charged that New Hampshire's resi-dents sympathized with abolitionist fanatics. As evidence for his accusation, Calhoun sent a newspaper clipping to the clerk's desk to be read. How Calhoun obtained this piece from the recently established *Herald of Freedom*, an abolitionist organ in Concord, is unclear, but the article said that Pierce had lied when he declared that only one person in five hundred in New

Hampshire sympathized with the abolitionists. By adding up the number of signatures on petitions from the state and dividing that sum by the state's population reported in the 1830 census, the *Herald of Freedom* claimed that the proper ratio was one in thirty-three. If Pierce was so ignorant of his constituency, the article added, he should resign. Significantly, this article also labeled Pierce a *doughface*, a term that subsequently connoted a northerner with southern sympathies, but in the North at the time it was an allegation of personal cowardice. Isaac Hill, New Hampshire's other senator, and Thomas Hart Benton immediately chastised Calhoun for allowing this slur against Pierce to be read on the Senate floor, and Calhoun later apologized to Pierce for having done so. But that apology was not enough for the furious Pierce, who had been in the Senate when the clipping was read.

On February 15 Pierce asked and received permission in the House "to repel an assault on his personal character, and impugning his veracity." The vast majority of the signatures on the petitions counted by the *Herald of Freedom*, he pointed out, came from women and children. His earlier speech had alluded only to white male voters. In recent months, he added, every county in New Hampshire had held conventions to nominate candidates for the impending state election in March, and every convention, regardless of party, had condemned the abolitionist petitioners for jeopardizing the Union. Finally, he angrily rejected the characterization of himself as a doughface. Pierce's indignant speech won plaudits from other congressmen and constituents in New Hampshire. The doughface label, however, was only temporarily shelved, not permanently buried.

In December 1836, after Pierce had returned to Washington for the second session of the Twenty-fourth Congress, the New Hampshire legislature elected him to the U.S. Senate for the six-year term beginning in March 1837. At the age of thirty-two, Pierce was the youngest man yet elected to the Senate but, according to the *Boston Post*, he had "more experience in legislative business than many of his seniors." The appointment kept Pierce in Washington for a few weeks after Congress adjourned, for the new Senate was charged with confirming the cabinet selections of the new president, Martin Van Buren, who was sworn into office on March 4, 1837.

Pierce again returned to Washington in September for a special session of Congress called by Van Buren to deal with the recession triggered by a banking panic in May 1837. Van Buren, like Pierce himself, attributed the panic to rampant speculation caused by an overissue of state banknotes, and his solution was to drastically reduce the amount of paper money in circulation. Van Buren proposed withdrawing federal monies from the private economic sector and depositing them in government vaults, known as subtreasuries, where they could no longer serve as backing for banknotes. Whigs and a minority of conservative Democrats opposed this so-called Independent Treasury plan, while orthodox Jacksonians like Pierce staunchly supported it. From September 1837 until July 1840, when Democrats finally managed to enact the Independent Treasury, this would remain the chief public policy question debated in Congress.

During Pierce's years in the Senate, the start of each session also rehashed the appropriate way to handle the continuing onslaught of abolitionist petitions. Indeed, Pierce's maiden Senate speech in December 1837 objected to a southern proposal for flat-out rejection. Abolitionists were dangerous fanatics, he repeated, but he "could give no vote that might be construed into a denial of the right of petition." Instead, he favored the kind of gag he had helped frame in the House in 1836— reception but then immediate tabling of the petitions without any discussion of their content.

As in the House, most of Pierce's time in the Senate was consumed by the drudgery of committee work. That routine was shattered by an incident outside the halls of Congress in early 1838. During the September special session, Pierce had shared a mess with his old Bowdoin chum Jonathan Cilley, now a freshman Democratic representative from Maine. When he returned to Washington for the regular session in December, this time with Jane in tow, he renewed that arrangement. Cilley was a firebrand, and in February he found himself challenged to a duel by Kentucky Whig congressman William J. Graves. Cilley consulted frequently with Pierce during the lead-up to the duel, which, at Cilley's request, would be fought with rifles at a distance of eighty yards. Some newspapers later charged that Pierce had goaded Cilley into fighting when in fact he unsuccessfully, if indirectly, tried to avert the duel. On February 24, 1838, Graves shot and killed Cilley, outraging the Washington community. Pierce was overwhelmed by guilt and grief, and Jane's hatred of politics and her husband's political career intensified. "Oh, how I wish he was out of political life!" she wrote a relative. "How much better it would be for him on every account."

That summer, after the close of the long congressional session, the Pierces moved from Hillsborough, where Jane had never been comfortable, to Concord, the state capital, where they rented a house and Pierce formed a new law partnership. Jane agreed to return to Washington for the second session of the Twenty-fifth Congress, but the birth of a healthy son, Frank Robert, in September 1839 gave her an excuse never to return there again during the remainder of his term.

· · ·

Still, the most important juncture during Pierce's senatorial years was the political earthquake that occurred in 1840 when

Whigs won the White House, three-fifths of the House seats, and two-thirds of the state legislatures, guaranteeing them a majority in the Senate as well. When Congress met on May 31, 1841, for the special session called by President William Henry Harrison before he died one month to the day after his inauguration, Pierce found himself in the minority for the first time in his precocious political career. He and other Democrats sat by powerlessly as Whigs, led by Henry Clay, whom many suspected had put Graves up to challenging Cilley, rammed through a package of economic legislation that the Democrat Pierce abhorred. Frustrated by his minority status, aware that he could not be reelected because New Hampshire's Democrats chose to rotate the state's Senate seats, determined to increase the income from his oft-interrupted law practice, and eager to be with Jane and his son, Pierce resigned his seat at the end of February 1842, a full year before his term was due to expire.

One other factor may have influenced Pierce's desire to escape Washington. In the early fall of 1841, while back in Concord after the close of the special congressional session, he had publicly taken the temperance pledge, and in 1842 he became president of the state temperance association. Alone without Jane in Washington's heavy-drinking culture, Pierce may have found the temptation to break that pledge too agonizing to bear. His return to Concord would help him avoid it.

Pierce had resigned from political office, but to Jane's growing dismay he most certainly had not left political life. Pierce served as the de jure and then de facto boss of New Hampshire's Democratic state party from 1842 until his nomination for the presidency in 1852. In that role he tried, usually with success, to resolve squabbles over issues as well as party nominations in order to preserve party unity. For Pierce, the unity of the Democratic Party, both within the state and within the nation as a whole, was a fixation, a shibboleth, virtually a be-all and end-all. His obsession with obtaining that unity would help wreck his presidency. But between 1842 and 1852 it primarily drove Pierce to extirpate any and every inkling of antislavery or antisouthern sentiment from the New Hampshire Democratic Party. He simply would not tolerate any criticism of slavery or slaveholders, and he had the clout to impose his intolerance on the state Democratic organization. On two occasions—in 1845 and then again in 1851—he called special sessions of the Democratic state convention and ordered members to oust previously nominated men from the state ticket because they had the temerity publicly to announce antislavery sentiments.

The first of these occasions was by far the more portentous. In 1843 Pierce's fellow Bowdoin alumnus John P. Hale had been elected to Congress on the Democratic slate. The state convention in June 1844 renominated Hale, but before the March 1845 elections Hale publicly denounced a central plank of the Democrats' 1844 national platform, one that many believed had spurred James K. Polk's ascent to the White House that year—the immediate annexation of the slaveholding Republic of Texas. Hale believed that adding Texas to the Union as a slave state would spread a sinful institution and tighten the grip of the so-called Slave Power on the national government. He was so firm in his stance that he voted against the Democrats when the question came before Congress in the winter of 1844–45. Once stripped of his Democratic nomination by the recalled Democratic state convention, the defiant Hale ran as an independent in 1845. Like most New England states, New Hampshire required an absolute majority rather than a plurality of the popular vote for election to all offices. In 1845 the votes of Hale's supporters combined with the Whigs managed to keep anyone from being elected to the seat, one that Pierce thought rightfully belonged to the Democrats.

Nor did the damage stop there. In 1846 Hale's antislavery supporters, Whigs, and Democrats all ran separate candidates for governor and the state legislature. No one gained a majority in the gubernatorial race, but in the state legislature Hale's supporters plus the Whigs attained a majority over the usually dominant Democrats. So they cut a deal. They elected the Whig candidate Anthony Colby, who had gotten about 37 percent of the popular vote, as governor, the only Whig ever to hold that office in New Hampshire, and they sent John P. Hale to the Senate for a term running from March 1847 to March 1853. Pierce was absolutely livid, and in 1847 he mobilized a huge increase in Democratic turnout that crushed the Whigs and Hale's allies, now running under the Liberty Party label, in the state and congressional elections. That smashing victory probably increased Pierce's confidence that antislavery men were a contemptible minority, but there was little he could do to stop Hale from becoming one of the most prominent antislavery politicians in the country. In 1852, indeed, Hale would be named a candidate for president of the United States on the antislavery Free Soil Party ticket.

Several aspects of Pierce's career until the mid-1840s provide clues to his subsequent behavior as president. One is the striking ease of his political ascent. On Pierce's part this was primarily attributable to his amiable personality and his astonishing memory for people's names and faces. He had, in short, the instincts of a clubhouse pol, and he was likely overconfident about his ability to win over others with his personal charm. Pierce was a good public speaker, in part because his memory allowed him to eschew written texts and notes, but there's no evidence that anything he said was deep or original. Both in the state legislature and in Congress he hewed closely to Democratic orthodoxy, and his only significant action in Congress was helping to frame the controversial Pinckney Gag

Rule. Not only did Pierce hold antislavery groups in contempt, but his consistent votes against federal subsidies for internal improvements and lower federal land prices displayed a callous indifference to the needs and interests of the Midwest. His political vision was narrow, even parochial.

Yet more important in explaining Pierce's precocious political career was the lock that the Democratic Party held over New Hampshire. Whig candidates rarely secured as much as two-fifths of the popular vote, and in 1836, 1840, and 1844 New Hampshire gave Democratic presidential candidates larger popular majorities than any other northern state. The atypicality of Democratic strength in New Hampshire probably deepened Pierce's commitment to internal party unity. Since the early 1820s, astute politicians had recognized that any party's internal cohesion varied inversely with the strength of its external rivals. Where that external competition was weak, as in New Hampshire, internal party fragmentation was a constant danger. Democratic dominance in New Hampshire also blinded Pierce to the needs of Democrats in far more competitive states. That Pierce resigned his Senate seat after spending only four months in the minority is telling. He liked to compete only when he held a winning hand. Political defeat was a new and intolerable experience.

Pierce's successful campaign for the presidency in 1852 and his actions while in that office would in many ways eerily echo his experience in the 1830s and 1840s. By 1852 the opposition Whigs had become as weak nationally as they had always been in New Hampshire. As a result, Pierce would waltz into the White House with a landslide in the electoral vote. On becoming president, however, Pierce would immediately face the problem of holding the victorious Democratic coalition together when the temporary lack of a threatening external opposition party made that goal difficult, if not impossible. The upshot would be a piece of legislation that Pierce prominently endorsed and that, along with other things, produced the Democratic defeats that Pierce could not stand. But to understand how this happened, one must first assess the impact of the Mexican-American War of 1846–48 on American politics in general and upon Franklin Pierce in particular.

2

War, Sectional Crisis, and Election

From mid-1846 until his election as president in November 1852, Pierce's life was primarily shaped by the course and consequences of a single event: the Mexican-American War. That war in turn was mainly the product of President James K. Polk's determination to annex the Mexican province of Upper California to the United States. When attempts to buy California from Mexico failed, Polk ordered troops commanded by Zachary Taylor to the northeastern bank, near the mouth of the Rio Grande, an area that Mexicans firmly believed was their own soil. After Mexican troops attacked Taylor's soldiers, as Polk had likely hoped, Polk used that assault to obtain what was in effect a declaration of war from the Democratic Congress in May 1846.

Pierce had befriended Polk during his two terms in the House when Polk was Speaker. He had worked hard in 1844 to mobilize New Hampshire's Democrats for Polk's election to the White House, and New Hampshire gave Polk a larger percentage of its vote than any other northern state. In gratitude for that achievement, Polk appointed Pierce as U.S. attorney for New Hampshire, and in August 1846 he invited him to serve in his cabinet as attorney general. Aware that Jane, who was mourning the death of their second son, Frank Robert, at the age of four, still loathed Washington, Pierce declined the offer, citing family responsibilities. He wanted no public office, he averred, while adding a significant caveat, "except at the call of my country in time of war."

Since boyhood Pierce had dreamed of reliving the military exploits of his father and older brothers. Yet Pierce did not rush off to war in 1846, largely because of his concern for Jane and a conviction that someone of his age and stature deserved a command in the regular army. That opportunity came in early 1847, when Congress called for the creation of ten additional regular army regiments. In February Polk appointed Pierce as a colonel and charged him with raising one of the new regiments in New Hampshire. On March 3 his commission was elevated to the rank of brigadier general to command a group of regiments from several New England states. Pierce's brigade would serve under General Winfield Scott, who planned to invade Mexico via the port of Vera Cruz. It took time to raise and equip the regiments, and Scott captured Vera Cruz while Pierce was still in New England. By the time Pierce reached that port on June 27, Scott had long since moved more than a hundred miles inland, where he awaited Pierce and his brigade as well as a wagon train of supplies for his army.

Pierce's immediate task in Vera Cruz, then, was to assemble transportation for Scott's supplies and then march the 2,500 men under his command as well as scores of wagons and a battery of heavy artillery through 150 miles of enemy territory to his rendezvous with Scott. On the route Pierce's men came under attack six times, and a few were wounded. The journey took twenty-one days, and Pierce displayed considerable skill and determination in accomplishing it. It was his finest achievement in Mexico, one that Scott would commend in his official dispatches to Washington.

The remainder of his brief military career, in contrast, was consistently luckless. The New Englanders under Pierce's command acquitted themselves quite well in a series of battles outside Mexico City, but personal glory eluded him. In his first serious battle, Pierce sat astride a horse given to him by his Concord townsmen and was ready to lead the brigade in a frontal assault on an enemy position. But a Mexican artillery salvo frightened Pierce's steed, causing it to buck and throwing Pierce's groin violently against the saddle pommel. Pierce briefly lost consciousness and began to fall from the saddle. His horse tripped and fell on Pierce's knee, resulting in a serious and painful injury. After Pierce recovered consciousness, he told his orderly to quickly secure one of his regimental commanders to lead the attack. But the damage to his leadership had been done. That Pierce had seemingly fainted in response to enemy fire inspired someone to shout, "Take command of the brigade. General Pierce is a damned coward."

In the brigade's next battle Pierce, safely on foot—or so he thought—twisted the same knee injured in the previous fall and collapsed in acute pain. Again his men marched by as their commander lay on the ground. This time Pierce managed to hobble after his men, but by the time he reached them the serious fighting had ended. Finally, Pierce's brigade took part in the storming of Chapultepec, the final battle of the entire campaign, but Pierce did not accompany them. He lay instead in a sick tent plagued with acute diarrhea.

Once Mexico City had fallen and it was clear serious fighting was over, Pierce grew increasingly bored with army life. He and his fellow officers formed a social club where much liquor was consumed, and where on one occasion a particularly drunken officer challenged Pierce to a duel, which he refused to fight. In these days of occupation duty, Pierce made some important friendships with men such as Gideon Pillow of Tennessee, John Claiborne and Pierre Beauregard of Louisiana, John A. Quitman

of Mississippi, James Shields of Illinois, Caleb Cushing of Massachusetts, and Thomas Seymour of Connecticut. All of these
men, not coincidentally, were fellow Democrats, and some of
them, particularly Pillow, detested their Whig commander, Winfield Scott. Pierce himself admired Scott, and the esteem was
mutual. He granted Pierce's request for a leave of absence, and
Pierce left Mexico in December 1847, arriving in New Orleans
on December 27, exactly six months after he had landed at Vera
Cruz. A hero's welcome awaited him when he reached Concord
in January, but he could not resign his commission until after
Senate ratification of the Treaty of Guadalupe Hidalgo, in March
1848, officially ended the war.

• • •

Well before that happened, it had become clear that "Mr. Polk's
War," as Whigs called it, would permanently alter American
political life. From the war's start Whigs across the nation, South
as well as North, had denounced it as an act of immoral aggression, a naked land grab. But in the North they had also leveled
the politically lethal charge that it was principally a slaveholders'
war fought for the extension of slavery beyond Texas, whose
annexation Whigs almost to a man had vainly tried to stop. In
part to defuse this northern Whig accusation, in early August
1846 a freshman Democratic congressman from Pennsylvania
named David Wilmot offered an amendment to an appropria-
tions bill sought by Polk. Famous thereafter as the Wilmot
Proviso, it would bar slavery from any territory to be acquired
from Mexico as a result of the war.

Wilmot's amendment instantly split both parties along
sharp sectional lines. In the House every southerner opposed
its adoption, while all but four northerners supported it. No
vote was taken on the amendment in the Senate, however, and
Congress adjourned without passing it. Nor would Congress

ever enact it, even though it would be repeatedly reintroduced over the next four years as sectional asperity over the prospect of congressional prohibition of slavery from western territories intensified. By 1849 fourteen of fifteen northern state legislatures, including New Hampshire's, had instructed their U.S. senators to impose the proviso on any territories formally organized in the West, and southern state after southern state had threatened to secede should Congress ever enact the proviso into law. Not all southerners believed that slavery could be profitably extended to the arid Southwest, but virtually all of them considered the proviso a slur on their honor, an intolerable violation of their equal rights in the nation. Thus Wilmot, by shifting sectional concerns from abolition to slavery's westward expansion, had engendered a dangerous sectional crisis.

Both Whigs and Democrats were now forced to find some way to avoid or finesse their sectional divisions over the Wilmot Proviso. The amendment dealt with a hypothetical situation. In the summer of 1846 almost everyone in Washington knew that Polk hoped to extort California from Mexico, but only three months into the war it was unclear that he could succeed. Thus for all of 1847 the great majority of northern and southern Whigs united behind a demand that no territory whatsoever be taken from Mexico as a result of the war. That way there would be no new territory into which slavery might expand and no area on which northerners could impose the insulting proviso. This politically ingenious stance became moot, however, with the ratification of the Treaty of Guadalupe Hidalgo. The treaty brought with it the enormous Mexican Cession, all the land area west of Texas and the Louisiana Territory between the thirty-second and forty-second parallels. That windfall ultimately led the badly divided Whig Party to nominate as its 1848 presidential candidate General Zachary Taylor, whose views on the proviso—and indeed on any prominent issue—were utterly unknown.

Whigs then ran a Janus-faced campaign. In the North they promised that Taylor would not veto the proviso; in the South, they promised that Taylor, who lived in Louisiana and owned more than a hundred slaves, would never betray his fellow southerners by signing the proviso into law.

For their part, Democrats, including Pierce, initially found it more difficult than did Whigs to agree on a position. Some urged extension of the 1820 Missouri Compromise line west to the Pacific coast, with slavery barred north of the parallel thirty-six degrees, thirty minutes and permitted south of it. Others rallied behind a formula known as *popular sovereignty* or congressional nonintervention. This would remove any decision about slavery in the territories from Congress and allow the actual settlers in a territory to make the determination. Popular sovereignty was the position of the Democrats' eventual presidential nominee in 1848, Senator Lewis Cass of Michigan, who had publicly pledged in late 1847 to veto the Wilmot Proviso should it pass Congress while he was president. The party's national platform that year, however, said nothing about the territorial question, in part because a minority of northern Democrats clung to the basic parameters of the proviso. The most important group of these dissidents was Martin Van Buren's wing of New York State's badly divided Democratic Party. But they also included New Hampshire's Democrats, who, fearful of more defections to Hale's Liberty Party, endorsed the proviso in every state platform from 1847 through 1849. As late as January 1850, the state's major Democratic newspaper, which was allied with Pierce politically, insisted that Congress bar slavery from the Mexican Cession.

• • •

This, then, was the political situation when Franklin Pierce returned to New Hampshire in early 1848. He devoted most of his time tending to his increasingly lucrative legal practice and to Jane and their remaining son Benjamin. In fact, Pierce joined his family in daily morning prayers. Nonetheless, with some allies in Concord who were dubbed the Concord Regency, he also began to slowly and forcefully reassert leadership over the state's Democratic Party.

Then in mid-1848, the political situation shifted once again. Zachary Taylor's nomination by the Whigs and Cass's nomination by the Democrats had proved too much for the most fervent supporters of the Wilmot Proviso in the North. In August 1848 they formed the Free Soil Party, which vowed to stop slavery expansion by congressional statute and to prevent the admission of additional slave states into the Union. To facilitate the creation of an antislavery party with a broader constituency than the more radical Liberty Party had attracted, John Hale, Pierce's nettlesome New Hampshire rival whom the Liberty men had nominated for president in 1847, willingly stepped aside. The Free Soilers instead nominated ex-president Martin Van Buren with Charles Francis Adams, leader of Massachusetts' so-called Conscience Whigs, as his running mate. How the nation should deal with slavery expansion had emerged as the central, though not the only, issue of the 1848 presidential election.

Despite a private invitation from New York to take a spot on the Free Soil ticket in 1848, Pierce never considered supporting his erstwhile hero Van Buren. Instead he heroically marshaled the biggest possible vote for Lewis Cass, a graduate of New Hampshire's Exeter Academy. His exertions helped Cass carry New Hampshire with an even larger proportion of the vote—55.4 percent—than Polk had amassed in 1844. With less than 30 percent of the popular vote, Taylor, in turn, ran more poorly in New Hampshire than in any other state in the nation. Nonetheless, Pierce had reason for pause. In New Hampshire,

Democratic defectors to the new Free Soil Party who had not already bolted earlier to the Liberty Party outnumbered Whig defectors by a five-to-one ratio.

Cass carried New Hampshire, but Taylor won the national election. The campaigning accomplished nothing toward resolving the sectional crisis over the question of slavery in the newly acquired Mexican Cession. Pierce—voluntarily out of office and with his party out of the White House—could simply watch from afar as events unfolded. How they did so largely explains why he was elected president in 1852, although they by no means explain why he received the Democratic Party's nomination in the first place.

To avert further sectional wrangling, President Taylor sought to finesse the territorial issue altogether. Through various agents he urged the residents of California and New Mexico to write constitutions and apply for immediate statehood to the new Thirty-first Congress as soon as it assembled in December 1849. The New Mexicans failed to do so, but Californians drafted a constitution that would bar slavery from the new state. When Congress opened, Taylor urged the legislators to admit California to statehood under the terms of its constitution and to do nothing about the remainder of the Mexican Cession until New Mexico applied for statehood as well. Taylor's scheme had no chance of passing the Democratic Congress, and it fell to Congress itself to devise a solution.

After ten months of contentious wrangling and scores of indecisive roll-call votes, Congress settled on the Compromise of 1850, a package of five separate bills rather than a single piece of legislation. The first admitted California as a free state along its modern boundaries. The second and third formally organized territorial governments for Utah and New Mexico under the Democrats' popular sovereignty formula instead of the Wilmot Proviso, and reduced the size of Texas, which had claimed the entire land area east of the Rio Grande, including Santa Fe, in return for which the federal government would assume responsibility for paying off Texas's bonded debt. The last two laws had nothing to do with the Mexican Cession but were included in the compromise package. One barred public slave auctions in the District of Columbia as northerners had long sought. The other was a much more rigorous Fugitive Slave Act that measurably increased southern slaveholders' chances of capturing runaway slaves in the North.

As important as the substance of the Compromise of 1850 was the peculiar pattern of voting on its five parts that emerged in the House and the Senate and the subsequent impact on state and congressional elections. Southern Whigs and most northern Democrats were the compromise's staunchest supporters. The opposition coalition consisted of northern Free Soilers, the vast majority of northern Whigs who refused to accept the organization of territories without the Wilmot Proviso, and most southern Democrats who considered the admission of California as a free state and the reduction of slaveholding Texas as egregious affronts to slaveholders' rights.

Despite the odd alignment in Congress, the compromise could never have passed had Zachary Taylor lived, but he died on July 9, 1850. Taylor's death brought New York's Millard Fillmore to the presidency, and after some hesitation Fillmore named Daniel Webster, a strong pro-compromise man, as his secretary of state. In early August, Fillmore and Webster publicly announced their support for the compromise package, but even before then they had privately pressured northern Whig senators and representatives to allow passage of the concessions to the South. As a result of their pressure, usually involving threats about federal patronage allotment, a sufficient number of northern Whigs abstained on crucial roll-call votes to allow the prosouthern compromise bills to pass. Then, in his annual message to Congress in December 1850, Fillmore proclaimed the compromise, including the Fugitive Slave Act, as a final settlement of the slavery issue and one that must not be tampered with. In addition, he and Webster exerted every effort to ensure enforcement of the Fugitive Slave Act in the North, where it was widely reviled.

The bizarre alignment of parties that had appeared in Congress during 1850 carried over to the state and congressional elections of 1850 and 1851. In virtually every northern state, including New Hampshire, Democrats quickly embraced the compromise as necessary to save the Union. At a pro-Union rally in Concord in December 1850, Pierce gave a powerful and long-remembered speech praising the compromise and iterating his undying devotion to "The Union! Eternal Union!" When during that same month John Atwood, the previously nominated Democratic gubernatorial candidate, published a letter criticizing the Fugitive Slave Act, Pierce helped recall the Democratic state convention to oust Atwood from the ticket.

Meanwhile, the vast majority of northern Whigs attacked the compromise for conceding too much to the South. They demanded repeal of the Fugitive Slave Act and imposition of the Wilmot Proviso on the new territories of Utah and New Mexico. Both publicly and privately, from Maine to Michigan, they lacerated Fillmore and Webster for their roles in securing passage of the bills. In most northern states, however, a minority of pro-administration, pro-compromise Whigs refused to support anti-compromise Whig candidates, allowing Democrats to make substantial gains in the elections those years. These intraparty fights would help cripple Whigs' chances in the presidential election of 1852.

The political pattern in the South in 1850 and 1851 was the mirror image of that in the North. Whig candidates happily praised the compromise because it had apparently buried the insulting proviso and Fillmore because he strained every nerve to see that the Fugitive Slave Act was enforced. By mid-1851, indeed, Whigs across the South demanded that Fillmore be made the party's presidential candidate in 1852, a call that was anathema to most northern Whigs, who already were touting General Winfield Scott as their man. In contrast, most southern Democratic political leaders denounced the compromise as a sell-out of Southern Rights, yet many traditionally Democratic nonslaveholding voters abstained rather than support such Democratic candidates, allowing a number of Whig victories in state and congressional races. In the three Deep South states of Georgia, Alabama, and Mississippi—where some Democratic leaders urged secession because California had been admitted as a free state, thereby upsetting the sectional balance in the Senate—a more fundamental political realignment occurred. Most Democrats joined new Southern Rights parties that seemed to advocate secession. But many nonslaveholding Democratic voters instead chose to combine with the Whigs in the new "Union" parties that defended the compromise and opposed secession.

Of vast importance, key Democratic leaders who acquiesced in the Compromise of 1850 joined with ancient Whig foes to lead these Union parties. In Georgia, for example, Howell Cobb, the Democratic Speaker of the House of Representatives, allied with Whigs Alexander H. Stephens and Robert Toombs to build a Union Party that not only crushed the drive for secession in 1850 but also elected Cobb governor and sent Toombs to the U.S. Senate in 1851. Mississippi's two Democratic senators squared off in the state's gubernatorial election of 1851. Henry S. Foote was the Union Party champion; Jefferson Davis, a key leader of the anti-compromise coalition in the Senate during 1850, represented the Southern Rights Party. In all three states, the Union Party won sweeping victories.

By the end of 1851, it was clear that continued opposition to the compromise was a political loser in the South just as it was in the North. Too many Democratic nonslaveholders in the South and too many conservative Whigs in the North refused to back their parties' candidates if they took an extremist position that threatened the settlement. In early 1852 both Whig and Democratic politicians dropped opposition to the compromise in an attempt to bring their abstainers and defectors back to the party fold. The upshot was that in 1852 both the Whig and the Democratic national platforms would in essence proclaim the Compromise of 1850 as the final settlement of the slavery issue. Democrats went so far as to pledge never again to allow a matter involving slavery to be raised in the halls of Congress. But for the political future of Franklin Pierce, one other decision was critical. Northern and southern Democratic leaders tacitly agreed that the only way to reunite their fractured party was to run a northerner for president in 1852.

. . .

By mid-1851, if not earlier, it was clear that 1852 was going to be a Democratic year. Northern and southern Whigs remained badly divided over the compromise and the identity of their candidate. As Whigs themselves admitted, an economic boom fueled by the California gold strikes and a surge of British investment had rendered Whigs' traditional economic platform—that active governmental support was necessary to achieve prosperity—obsolete. With a Democratic victory apparently certain, infighting for the Democratic nomination began in late 1850 and continued until the national convention in June 1852. Seeking the prize were New York's William L. Marcy; Kentucky's William O. Butler, the Democrats' vice presidential candidate in 1848; and New Hampshire's Levi Woodbury, a Supreme Court associate justice whom the state party endorsed in June

1851. But the three main contenders were Lewis Cass, the 1848 standard-bearer; Pennsylvania's James Buchanan, the secretary of state in Polk's administration and a particular favorite of southern Democrats; and Illinois senator Stephen A. Douglas, who had successfully guided the compromise measures through the Senate in August 1850.

Douglas was the favorite of a younger generation of Democrats, known as Young America, who publicly blasted men like Cass, Buchanan, and Marcy as "old fogies" and demanded that the party now turn to "young blood, young ideas, [and] young hearts." Needless to say, such intemperate rhetoric turned the supporters of older candidates against Douglas's pretensions. Young America, significantly, also demanded that the United States embrace a much more aggressive foreign and commercial policy than had been pursued by the Taylor and Fillmore administrations. Relations among the three front-runners had become so rancorous by the summer of 1851 that many Democratic politicians began to wonder openly if any of them could possibly achieve the two-thirds majority necessary for nomination at the Democratic national convention.

Then, in September 1851, Levi Woodbury died, instantly elevating Franklin Pierce to the status of New Hampshire's favorite son. In January 1852 the Democratic state convention touted his qualifications for the presidency and recommended "his name to the people of the nation as worthy . . . of a high place among the names of the eminent citizens, who will be conspicuously before the National Democratic Convention." Such talk appalled Jane, and Pierce replied in a public letter to Charles Atherton, the state convention's chairman, "The use of my name in any event before the Democratic National Convention at Baltimore . . . would be utterly repugnant to my tastes and wishes." Yet the same paper, the *New Hampshire Patriot*, that published his letter added, "We do not understand from his letter that he forbids the use of his name entirely . . . or that he would decline a nomination tendered him by the great party to which he belongs."

That winter New Hampshire's Democratic congressmen began to spread the word privately in Washington that Pierce would be an ideal compromise candidate should the party's convention deadlock as was then widely expected. The state contingent was aided by Sidney Webster, who had once clerked in Pierce's law office, and by his old friend Benjamin French. Soon others joined in this propaganda campaign, particularly men Pierce had befriended in Mexico: Caleb Cushing, Connecticut's governor Thomas Seymour, and Gideon Pillow, who apparently envisaged Pierce as a running mate on a ticket he himself would head.

The Pierce lobbyists confronted two obstacles in their efforts. First, word reached Washington that in January Pierce had given a speech in which he stated that he disliked the Fugitive Slave Act and considered portions of it inhumane. Nonetheless, he had added, it must be obeyed as part of the compromise package. Such talk hardly endeared Pierce to southern Democrats. Pierce's friends countered it by describing his firm actions against Hale and Atwood in response to their antislavery heresies. Also looming was Pierce's public letter to Atherton renouncing any interest in running, for regardless of what the *New Hampshire Patriot* opined, that seemed a definitive extinguisher. Thus, in April both French and Edmund Burke, a Democratic editor from New Hampshire, sent letters pleading that Pierce allow his name to be used. Burke added that the best strategy would be to wait for the three front-runners to sink one another before a word about Pierce was uttered at the convention in Baltimore. To this strategy, Pierce agreed. The situation had changed since January, Pierce wrote to Burke. "If you and my other discreet friends think . . . that

the pride of our State, the success of the cause can be sub-served by the use of my name then you must judge for me in view of all the circumstances." Without ever telling Jane of his ambition, Pierce had given his supporters the green light.

Shortly before the Democratic convention met in early June, Pierce seized an opportunity to reassure southerners about his fidelity to the Compromise of 1850 and especially to the Fugitive Slave Act. A Richmond, Virginia, editor had asked him if he would do everything in his power to sustain that law and veto any attempt to repeal or revise it. Rather than writing a direct response, Pierce sent a letter to a Maine delegate to the Baltimore convention who could circulate it privately. Northerners must not insist on any platform plank offensive to the South, he maintained. "Having fought the battle in New Hampshire upon the fugitive slave law and upon what we believed to be the ground of constitutional right, we should of course desire the approval of the democracy of the country. . . . If the compromise measures are not to be substantially and firmly maintained, the plain rights secured by the constitution will be trampled in the dust. . . . If we of the North, who had stood by the constitutional rights of the South, are to be abandoned by any time-serving policy, the hopes of the democracy and of the Union must sink together."

• • •

The Democratic national convention opened in Baltimore on Wednesday, June 1, and balloting for the presidential nominee began the following day. Through thirty-three ballots on Thursday and Friday, with the New Hampshire delegation scattering its votes, the lead seesawed back and forth among Cass, Buchanan, and Douglas, but no one came close to the necessary two-thirds majority. At a strategy session on Friday night, the Buchanan delegates made a crucial decision. Pennsylvania, Georgia, and

Alabama would continue to back Buchanan on Saturday, but North Carolina and Mississippi would switch to Marcy on the next ballot. Virginia, at the insistence of Henry Wise, who had been lobbied intensely by Benjamin French and Caleb Cushing and shown the letter Pierce sent to the Maine delegate, would vote for Pierce. The objective, apparently, was to demonstrate that no other candidate could garner a two-thirds majority so the convention would turn back in Buchanan's favor. Instead, the result of this decision was Pierce's nomination.

On Saturday's first roll call, the convention's thirty-fourth ballot, Virginia staged a ruse and voted for Daniel S. Dickinson, the leader of the Cass forces at the convention, who immediately refused to be considered. Then on the next ballot Virginia cast fifteen votes for Pierce, the first time his name had been publicly mentioned on the convention floor. With the next ballot New Hampshire and Maine joined Virginia, bringing Pierce's total to twenty-nine. There he stood until the forty-sixth ballot when Kentucky added its fifteen votes to his total. A few more delegates from Maryland and Massachusetts swung to his column on the next two ballots. French persuaded Dickinson to bring the New York delegates on board, if he could. The roll calls proceeded in geographic, not alphabetical, order, from the northernmost to the southernmost states. On the forty-ninth ballot nothing changed until James C. Dobbin, the chairman of the North Carolina delegation that had been pledged to Buchanan, praised Pierce's fidelity to the Constitution and the Compromise of 1850 and cast the state's votes for him. Dobbin's move set off a landslide in Pierce's direction. By the end of the ballot Pierce had 202 votes, Cass and Douglas two votes each, and Kentucky's Butler a single vote.

In its remaining hours the convention nominated William R. King of Alabama, a strong ally of Buchanan, for vice president and adopted the party's platform. Its key planks pledged that

Democrats would abide by the Compromise of 1850, including the Fugitive Slave Act, "which act being designed to carry out an express provision of the Constitution, cannot, with fidelity thereto, be repealed, or so changed as to destroy its efficiency," and that the party "will resist all attempts at renewing, in Congress or out of it, the agitation of the slavery question under whatever shape or color the attempt may be made."

Pierce and his wife had spent the week of the convention in Boston, and that Saturday they had gone on a carriage ride to Cambridge. On their return trip they were met by a horseback rider with the news that Pierce had been nominated. Pierce seemed stunned. Jane fainted dead away.

Just like the delegates at Baltimore, Democrats around the country quickly rallied around the dark horse nominee. Pro-compromise Democrats from the Deep South had abandoned the Union Party even before the convention and were delighted with the platform. But southern Democrats who had denounced the compromise for two years were just as pleased with the candidate and the platform's commitment to the finality of the Fugitive Slave Act. Northern Democrats had been primarily divided over men, not the compromise, and Cass, Buchanan, Douglas, and Marcy soon pledged their support to Pierce. So did former Free Soilers like Martin Van Buren's son. The chief organ of Young America crowed that "a generation is passing away" and "Young America . . . is about to rule."

The Whigs' response to Pierce's nomination was, predictably, far less friendly. Southern Whig papers dismissed Pierce as an "obscure and unknown individual." Philadelphia's main Whig sheet tried to alienate midwestern Democrats from Pierce by pointing out correctly that Pierce, while in Congress, had voted against every single internal improvements bill that had come to the floor. The Whig-affiliated *Boston Atlas* attributed Pierce's nomination exclusively to "his complete and abject devotion to the demands of the South. No man has ever earned for himself more deservedly the reputation of a most thorough-paced dough-face."

Many Whig newspapers also jumped on Pierce's role as president of a state constitutional convention held in Concord from November 1850 until mid-January 1851 that sought to revise the original state constitution adopted in 1782. Altogether fifteen changes were submitted to the state's electorate in March 1851, but the most important was the elimination of a provision in the old constitution that barred Roman Catholics from holding any public office in the state. Pierce spoke passionately in favor of this change on the convention floor, yet voters rejected it by a five-to-one margin. Because Pierce had presided over the constitutional convention and because the heavily Democratic state had overwhelmingly refused to replace the anti-Catholic provision, upon Pierce's nomination for president Whig papers loudly, if falsely, also charged that he was an anti-Catholic bigot. "To Your Tents, Catholics!" blared Whig headlines.

Yet if Whigs could unite in mocking Pierce, they could unite on little else. For months prior to the meeting of the Whig national convention in Philadelphia on June 13, southern Whig congressmen and newspapers had vowed that they could never support General Winfield Scott, the favorite for the nomination, unless he issued a written public pledge, before the convention, to the finality of the Compromise of 1850 and of the Fugitive Slave Act in particular. By 1852 Scott's northern Whig managers no longer had any intention of running against the compromise, but they dearly wanted to stop any pledge about the compromise coming from Scott or appearing in the party's platform. Silence, they believed, would be enough to attract northern antislavery men. As a result, Scott declared nothing prior to the convention. At the convention itself, supporters of Fillmore and Webster, who insisted on a

platform commitment to finality, had a majority, and the platform they wanted won easy adoption. But the Fillmore and
Webster delegates refused to combine behind the other man,
and after fifty-two ballots Scott was nominated, with North
Carolina's William A. Graham as his running mate. Almost
instantly, nine southern Whig congressmen publicly stated that
they could not support Scott, and it was immediately clear that
Scott would be crushed at the polls in the Deep South. Meanwhile, Horace Greeley, editor of the *New York Tribune*, the most
influential Whig newspaper in the North, expressed most northern Whigs' opinion of the platform: "We defy it, execrate it,
spit upon it." These sectional divisions along with the obsoles-
cence of the Whigs' economic platform vastly enhanced Pierce's
chances of victory.

Whig efforts to court Catholic voters and to focus the election
on the personalities of the candidates failed to blunt that edge.
"Hero of many a well fought bottle," Whigs whispered about
Pierce, and others publicly rehearsed charges of his apparent
cowardice in Mexico. Nothing worked. Wooing Catholic immigrants alienated normal Protestant Whig voters. Slurs about
Pierce, who followed tradition and did no personal campaigning,
failed. The cold fact was that no issues separated the parties, and
the Democrats had gained the momentum since Taylor's election
in 1848. The electorate was distinctly unenthused. "General
Apathy is the strongest candidate out here," wrote a wag from
Cincinnati, while a frustrated Whig campaigner from western
Pennsylvania complained that trying to mobilize Whig voters
"was something like pissing against the wind, when blowing sixty
miles to the hour." Nationally, the turnout rate was the lowest
since the election of 1836, and it would remain the lowest turnout rate until the 1920s. Abstention by normal Whig voters was
especially prevalent in the Deep South.

The result was a rout that even Whigs called "a Waterloo

defeat." Pierce carried all but four states: Vermont, Massachusetts, Kentucky, and Tennessee. He thus overwhelmed Scott in the electoral vote, 254 to 42. He captured almost 51 percent of the popular vote to Scott's 44 percent, while John P. Hale, the antislavery, anti-compromise Free Soil candidate, got only 5 percent of the national total. Hale, in fact, barely attracted half as many votes as Van Buren had in 1848, and he exceeded 10 percent of the total statewide vote in only four northern states, one of them his native New Hampshire, where Pierce amassed 57 percent of the vote. In addition, Democrats won 61 percent of the North's congressional seats filled in 1852, and they would win all of them filled in 1853. In contrast, only four Free Soilers won election to Congress. The nation's electorate had apparently spoken emphatically. It wanted no tampering with the Compromise of 1850, no further agitation of the slavery issue, and no part of the party that hoped to keep the slavery issue alive.

3

No "Timid Forebodings of Evil from Expansion"

The rout of the Whigs in 1852, a rout that only worsened in 1853, established a national political landscape akin to that of New Hampshire—overwhelming Democratic dominance. Astute observers recognized immediately that this lopsidedness increased the chances of Democratic fragmentation. In late November, the Washington correspondent of a northern Whig newspaper opined that "the overthrow of the Whig party is so complete and the triumph of our opponents so perfect that Genl. Pierce will be greatly embarrassed to preserve the friendship and retain the adherence of the various and conflicting sections of his own party." Pierce's inaugural address and his cabinet selections, he went on, were bound to provoke dissent from one section of the party or another. Hence, "that there will be an organized opposition arrayed against him in his own camp before the next Congress ends admits of little doubt." The following month the Tennessee Democrat Andrew Johnson echoed, "The Whig party is now disbanded leaving the [Democratic] party without external pressure to keep it together." Because few issues had separated the parties in 1852, he added, Pierce's administration "comes into power to carry out no Set of measures, nothing in fact to bind the party together with except the *'cohesive ties of public plunder'* which will soon give out." Or as the Whig *Raleigh Register* put it in January 1853, "When a political party gets into power by the success of various national factions . . . it may naturally be expected that all those factions will not sit down in celestial concord and sing anthems in honor of the individual whom they have elected. Faction contains a great deal of *latent* caloric."

Franklin Pierce fully comprehended the threat, and preserving the unity of the national Democratic Party became his top priority as president. Though all elements of the party had rallied behind his candidacy in 1852, internal divisions had rent Democrats in 1850 and 1851. In the North, a minority of the party had sought coalitions with antislavery Free Soilers in order to capture state governments, an aim that necessitated denunciation of the gingerly negotiated Compromise of 1850, while a majority had defended the compromise. In the South, in turn, a majority of Democrats had denounced the compromise as a sell-out of Southern Rights—southerners themselves always capitalized this phrase—while a minority had defended the compromise. Such internal divisions had been especially rancorous in Georgia, Alabama, and Mississippi, but they had existed almost everywhere across the region. On top of this hurdle, of course, the majority of Democratic politicians had initially supported other leaders—not Pierce—for the 1852 nomination. Those men, too, had to be appeased.

Understandably, therefore, constructing a party-unifying cabinet headed Pierce's agenda. Two goals initially shaped his thinking. First, as Pierce wrote James Buchanan, James K. Polk's secretary of state, in December, he had no intention of appointing any members of Polk's cabinet to his own. Second, and very much against Buchanan's advice, he was determined to share cabinet positions and subcabinet jobs across every faction of the party, not just among those Democrats who had always supported the Compromise of 1850 to which the party platform had been pledged. When Virginia's Henry Wise learned of this intention from a New Hampshire Democrat familiar with Pierce's plans, he protested, "I tell you *flatly* that if he makes such a botch of appointments as you conjecture, he won't have the confidence of Virginia long."

Pierce understood the difficulty of his aim. At first he hoped to anchor the cabinet on polar opposites: John A. Dix of New York, who had been the Free Soil candidate for governor there in 1848, and Senator Robert M. T. Hunter of Virginia, a vociferous defender of Southern Rights. This plan quickly aborted. Hunter refused to leave the Senate, and southern Democrats made it absolutely clear that they would block Dix at any cost. As recompense for his lost cabinet seat, Pierce promised to name Dix as minister to France, but southerners obstructed that appointment as well.

Stymied, Pierce fixed on two other men who might provide the sectional and factional balance he hoped to achieve. The first was Caleb Cushing of Massachusetts, Pierce's old Mexican-American War comrade to whom he had grown increasingly close during the maneuvering for the presidential nomination. Cushing was stridently pro-compromise, and he had led a minority wing of the Massachusetts Democratic Party that denounced its notorious coalition with Free Soilers that had sent the Free Soiler Charles Sumner to the Senate in 1851. Cushing, a onetime Whig and close friend of the now deceased Daniel Webster, would become Pierce's attorney general. Whig newspapers quickly dubbed him the "Magnus Apollo" of the administration. To offset that choice, Pierce wanted Mississippi's Jefferson Davis, a leader of the Senate's anti-compromise bloc in 1850 and that state's Southern Rights candidate for governor in 1851. But Pierce would not speak with Davis directly until after his inauguration in March.

. . .

In late December 1852, Jane's beloved uncle Amos Lawrence, who was especially fond of the Pierces' eleven-year-old son Benjamin, died of a stroke. The family went down to Boston for the funeral and planned to return to Concord via Andover, where they stayed with relatives for a few days. On January 6, 1853, they boarded a train consisting of a single passenger car for the short run to Concord, but about a mile out of the Andover station, the car derailed and tumbled down a twenty-foot culvert, landing on its roof. Pierce, who had been sitting next to Jane, was badly bruised, but alive, as was Jane. But Benny, who had been sitting alone on the seat behind them, had the back of his head sheared off and died instantly. Father and mother had to view this ghastly sight, and both were badly shaken. Jane was so undone, indeed, that she remained in Andover rather than come to Concord for the funeral. Nor would she travel to the capital for Pierce's inauguration.

Jane, accompanied by her cousin Abby Means, eventually arrived in Washington, eighteen days after the inauguration. She spent most of her time in seclusion while her cousin served as hostess at the many dinner parties Pierce held for congressmen and the diplomatic corps. It would not be until the end of 1854 that Jane herself appeared at the dinners.

Grief-ridden and hobbled by injuries, Pierce did not return his thoughts to cabinet making until early February. He moved then with some dispatch, for he had just one month to name his advisers. Thus, against his original intention, but at the strong urging of Buchanan and others, Pierce named New York's William L. Marcy, the secretary of war in Polk's administration and a rival for the 1852 nomination, as his secretary of state. A man of considerable political experience and ability, Marcy headed the so-called Soft-Shell faction of the New York Democracy. As such, he was an ally of Dix but the bitter foe of Daniel S. Dickinson, leader of the Hard-Shell faction, who as a senator in 1850 had done as much as any man to secure passage of the compromise. Both of these factions fully supported the compromise; they differed instead over the desirability of readmitting the Barnburner bolters of 1848 back into the good graces of the state's Democratic Party. This split would soon have significant ramifications for the administration. Pierce also sought to appease two other rivals for the 1852 nomination with his cabinet selections. For secretary of the interior, he chose Robert McClelland of Michigan, an ally of Lewis Cass and thus, at least nominally, a pro-compromise man. At Buchanan's request, he appointed James Campbell, an Irish Catholic from Philadelphia and a loyal adherent of Buchanan's wing of Pennsylvania's splintered Democratic Party, as postmaster general. Time would soon show that this appointment too had adverse political consequences for the administration. Pierce's selection for the Navy Department was North Carolina's James C. Dobbin, the man who had started the landslide in Pierce's direction at the Democratic convention. Pierce apparently believed that Dobbin was a firm pro-compromise man but, in fact, he, like the majority of North Carolina Democrats, had denounced the compromise as an affront to the South. Finally, for secretary of the treasury, Pierce picked James Guthrie of Kentucky, a businessman, and not a politician, who was highly recommended but entirely unknown to him. Pierce felt assured that after the inauguration Jefferson Davis would accept appointment as secretary of war.

Carefully balanced by region, Pierce's cabinet would prove to be one of the most ethical and effective group of advisers to serve the nation in the nineteenth century. It was also the only cabinet during that century to remain intact for an entire four-year presidential term. By the end of the administration, the cabinet members had developed genuine esteem for Pierce, and some, like Davis and Marcy, possessed personal fondness for him. Nonetheless, the cabinet contained only one man who had vigorously defended the Compromise of 1850 during the political warfare of 1850 and 1851 (Cushing) and two who had openly denounced it (Davis and Dobbin). Notably absent was any overt southern defender of the compromise. More important, with the exception of Guthrie, each of these men had Democratic factional rivals within his home state who howled at his selection.

Further, Pierce's cabinet selections sought a rapprochement of sorts with all but one of his competitors for the Democratic nomination, Stephen A. Douglas, the darling of Young America. Pierce attempted to rectify that slight with his subcabinet-level appointments, which ignited even more internal party discontent than those for the cabinet and with his policies. As the president-elect mulled over what he wanted to do in office, he settled on two priorities. In addition to making the bureaucratic administration of the executive branch more honest and efficient than it had been under his Whig predecessors, he would adopt a much more aggressive foreign policy, one in tune with the Young America wing of the party.

With Jane sequestered in Andover, Pierce traveled to Washington with only his personal secretary, Sidney Webster. At his inauguration on March 4, 1853, he astonished the crowd by delivering his carefully prepared address without once glancing at the notes that he held next to his thigh. "It is a relief to feel that no heart but my own can know the personal regret and bitter sorrow over which I have been borne to a position so suitable for others rather than desirable for myself," Pierce began. He then pledged to run a scrupulous administration, observe a strict construction of the Constitution, prevent a concentration of power in the central government, enforce the nation's neutrality laws, and adhere to the Monroe Doctrine's opposition to any further attempts by European powers at colonization in the western hemisphere. What is more, he vowed, in a clear bow toward Young America, "The policy of my Administration will not be controlled by any timid forebodings of evil from expansion. Indeed, it is not to be disguised that our attitude as a nation and our position on the globe render the acquisition of certain possessions not within our jurisdiction eminently important for our protection, if not in the future essential for the preservation of the rights of commerce."

Pierce closed his message by alluding to slavery and the Compromise of 1850. "I believe that involuntary servitude as it exists in different States of this Confederacy is recognized by the Constitution. . . . I hold that the laws of 1850, commonly called the 'compromise measures' are strictly constitutional and to be unhesitatingly carried into effect." Thus, he promised, his administration would rigorously enforce the Fugitive Slave Act. "I fervently hope that the [slavery] question is at rest," he closed, "and that no sectional or fanatical excitement may again threaten the durability of our institutions or obscure the light of our prosperity."

With the exception of that last "hope," Pierce's inaugural address provided a remarkably accurate blueprint for his time in office. Much to the frustration of many Democrats, he repeatedly vetoed internal improvements bills because he deemed them unconstitutional. The very first veto he cast nixed a bipartisan bill, long sought by the reformer Dorothea Dix, which would have provided federal funds to states to build and operate asylums for the indigent insane. "I cannot find any authority in the Constitution for making the Federal Government the great

almoner of public charity throughout the United States," wrote
Pierce. Such a scheme was "subversive of the whole theory upon
which the Union of these States is founded." With mixed success
Pierce also tried to enforce neutrality laws to prevent American
filibusters, as they were called, from invading foreign countries.
He scuttled several proposed expeditions against the Spanish
island of Cuba, but federal authorities in San Francisco failed to
stop the then-obscure and now-famous Tennessean William
Walker from sailing with a band of men to invade and ultimately
take control of Nicaragua.

. . .

While Congress was out of session between March and December 1853, Pierce's administration focused primarily on foreign
policy, and many of his plans remained concealed from the
press. In April, before he had picked any of his diplomatic team
for foreign posts, Vice President William R. King died at his
plantation home after a vain attempt to restore his health in
Cuba. Between his nomination and his election, Pierce had
never communicated with King, and had King lived he would
have undoubtedly had little impact on Pierce's policies. His
death, however, meant that the president pro tempore of the
Senate, Missouri Democrat David R. Atchison, stood next in
line for the succession, a fateful change in leadership as time
would show.

With new foreign policy initiatives his primary objective in
1853, Pierce devoted much of his focus after his inauguration
to staffing the diplomatic corps. For several key posts, Pierce
maintained his approach of preserving intraparty balance. To
Paris, Pierce eventually dispatched the aged Virginian John Y.
Mason, who had served in John Tyler's cabinet. Former senator
Solomon Downs of Louisiana, who had campaigned openly in
defense of the compromise in 1850 and 1851, won a post in

Latin America. August Belmont, an Austrian-born Jew who was the American agent of the Rothschild banking firm and who would serve as chairman of the Democrats' national committee between 1860 and 1872, went to The Hague. All of these were safe choices, and Belmont's was especially inspired.

From Pierce's perspective, however, relations with Mexico, Great Britain, and Spain were most at issue that year. When Pierce announced that he had no fear of territorial acquisition, one of the targets he had in mind was the area of northern Mexico south of New Mexico Territory, an area that seemed necessary for the completion of any transcontinental railroad to the Pacific coast along a southern route. To arrange for the purchase of this area, Pierce dispatched the South Carolinian James Gadsden, a seasoned railroad promoter, as minister to Mexico. Gadsden was also instructed to obtain the elimination of a provision in the Treaty of Guadalupe Hidalgo that obliged the U.S. Army to protect Mexico from Indian raids launched from New Mexico Territory.

When Gadsden reported to Washington that the Mexican president Santa Anna was desperate for cash, the administration authorized an offer of $50 million for a grandiose swath of northern Mexico and all of Lower California. Much to Pierce's disappointment, Gadsden ultimately purchased a much smaller section for $15 million, and the Senate would reduce that area still further when it finally ratified Gadsden's treaty, after first rejecting it, in the spring of 1854. Nonetheless, the Gadsden Purchase of 1853 filled out the land area of the continental United States.

· · ·

Rocky relations with Great Britain were a much higher priority for the administration, and they would take much longer to work out. Here, two problems—to the north and south of the

United States—seemingly became entangled. British naval vessels had been harassing New England fishermen seeking access to the waters off Nova Scotia and Newfoundland, and Pierce was eager to stop the harassment and gain greater access for his fellow New Englanders. As an inducement to the British, he hoped to work out a reciprocal trade agreement between Canada and the United States that would free certain goods from tariff duties. At the same time, Pierce was working to secure the trans-isthmian route in Central America by which most Americans traveled to the West Coast. In 1850 Zachary Taylor's secretary of state, John M. Clayton, had negotiated a treaty with Sir Henry Bulwer in which the United States and Great Britain agreed never to exercise exclusive control over or fortify any shipping canal built across Nicaragua and to keep any such canal open to shipping by both nations. More important in the near term, both nations pledged not to colonize, occupy, or exercise dominion over any part of Central America. By 1853 Americans believed that the British had violated this last provision by establishing new outposts on the coast of Central America, whereas the British contended that all of their possessions there antedated the Clayton-Bulwer Treaty and thus did not violate it.

After months of negotiation once he became president, Pierce persuaded James Buchanan to accept the post of minister to Great Britain, an assignment that more than anything else would help Buchanan win the Democratic Party's presidential nomination in 1856. When Pierce first approached Buchanan about serving as minister to the Court of Saint James, Buchanan insisted that he negotiate both issues so that he could use the carrot of a reciprocity treaty with Canada to entice the British to give up some of the possessions they claimed in Central America. Pierce, however, wanted Secretary of State Marcy to negotiate the Canadian matters with the

British minister in Washington while Buchanan worked on the Central American dispute in London. Buchanan balked at first but finally relented to the division of labor.

During the summer of 1853, Marcy and the British minister, John Crampton, made good progress in drafting a treaty concerning Canadian fisheries and trade. Yet it confronted two hurdles that delayed completion of the treaty and its Senate ratification until the spring of 1854. One was British insistence that Canadian coal be added to the list of products that could enter the United States duty-free, a provision ardently opposed by American coal producers in Pennsylvania and elsewhere. The other was getting approval of the treaty, not just from the U.S. Senate and British Parliament, but also from the individual parliaments of the various Canadian provinces. To facilitate that latter approval, Pierce appointed Israel Andrews, who had a long record of business dealings with Canadians, and procured a federal appropriation that Andrews could spend on propaganda pieces to be placed in Canadian newspapers. It seems clear, however, that Andrews spent that money—and much more than Congress appropriated, for which he would later unsuccessfully seek federal reimbursement—simply to bribe members of the various provincial parliaments. Finally, when Canadian coal was added to the free list in 1854, a treaty was signed and won ratification from the necessary bodies. Some historians have called this reciprocity treaty the signal diplomatic achievement of Pierce's administration.

Meanwhile, Buchanan, who did not reach England until the fall of 1853, had far less success in persuading the British to renounce dominion over their outposts on the coast of Central America that the United States believed violated the Clayton-Bulwer Treaty. Much of the delay related to the American personnel in London. As part of his campaign to include the Young America faction in his foreign policy team, Pierce had allowed several loose cannons to join the delegation. The appointment of George Sanders, the *Democratic Review* editor who had denounced Cass and Buchanan as "old fogies" in 1852, as consul in London and of Daniel Sickles as secretary of the legation there quickly proved embarrassing. Sanders hosted a series of widely publicized dinner parties for European revolutionaries including Louis Kossuth, Giuseppe Mazzini, and Giuseppe Garibaldi, who were then living in exile in London, dinners at which there was a great deal of talk about reigniting the revolutions of 1848. These gatherings deeply offended the British government and press. Thus Buchanan got nowhere in persuading the British to give up some of the possessions they claimed on the Central American coast throughout 1854 and 1855.

Then Pierce personally intervened. He devoted most of his third annual message, which was to go to Congress in December 1855, to the American case that the British had violated the Clayton-Bulwer Treaty, although it is not clear whether Pierce himself or Marcy wrote these sections of the message. But the congressional session was delayed by a prolonged election for Speaker of the House, frustrating Pierce's goal of delivering the message and having it published in Great Britain before the year closed. Finally, at the end of 1855, Pierce took the unusual and highly controversial step of sending the message to the Senate even before the House was officially organized. Fortunately, Buchanan soon reported to Marcy that Pierce's carefully argued message had impressed the British authorities, who were now ready to rethink their policy in Central America.

A more immediate crisis with the British had arisen, however. Britain and France went to war with Russia over the Crimea in 1854. The war soon proved to be a bonanza for American farmers, since Russia, along with the United States, had been the primary source of wheat imports into Britain.

Now Americans had a monopoly on that lucrative trade. Yet the war also occasioned a diplomatic spat, when British consuls in three American cities tried to recruit American residents for the British army and navy in violation of American neutrality laws. The Pierce administration immediately protested, and ultimately it expelled the three consuls as well as Crampton, fully expecting that the British would retaliate by expelling Buchanan from London. But the British government found the president's message so compelling, according to Buchanan, that it did not do so. Pierce had helped resolve a long-simmering quarrel with the world's most powerful nation.

· · ·

The administration's most fractious foreign relations were with Spain. And it was to Spain that Pierce sent his most conse-quential and unfortunate choice from the Young America fac-tion as minister: Pierre Soulé of Louisiana. A French émigré and fierce anti-compromise opponent of Downs and Senator John Slidell, Soulé almost instantly became persona non grata in Madrid, a particularly disturbing situation when relations with Spain fractured over the activities of Spanish officials in that country's possession, Cuba. For decades American politi-cians and bureaucrats had dreamed of annexing Cuba to the United States, and Pierce certainly shared their aspiration. Some prominent Americans feared that Spain might transfer possession of Cuba to Great Britain or France, in which case it could pose a serious threat to coastal shipping lanes and national security. Others voraciously eyed the sugar-producing wealth of the island. Many southern slaveholders envisioned that adding a new slave state to the Union would increase the South's political clout in Washington.

The Spanish, however, showed no intention of giving up Cuba. Instead, they had increased their military and naval forces on the island. Several years earlier, President Polk had offered to buy Cuba for $100 million but had been firmly rebuffed. During the Taylor and Fillmore administrations various filibustering expeditions to Cuba attempted to pursue another path. They mistakenly believed that resident planters in Cuba itched to rebel against Spanish authorities and that the landing of armed bands of Americans would ignite the revolution. In short, their model was Texas—first a successful revolution against the mother country and then eventual annexation to the United States. But these expeditions were fiascos, resulting in the humiliating flight of the filibusters' ships back to the United States or, in the case of those who gained landfall, execution by Spanish firing squads. So despite the fact that Pierce dearly wanted to acquire Cuba, neither he nor Marcy had any idea how to do so. As a result, Marcy gave no instructions about Cuba to Pierre Soulé when he sent him off to Madrid in 1853.

Soulé's tenure was inauspicious from the start. Within months of his arrival in the Spanish capital, he fought a duel with the French minister. By late 1853 relations over Cuba had grown tense. A new Spanish military governor-general arrived in Cuba and declared his intention to free the planters' slaves, an announcement that shocked many southern slaveholders. They worried that the step would lead to the Africanization of the island, turning it into another Haiti, and they increased pressure on Pierce to acquire Cuba by whatever means. Then, in February 1854, Spanish authorities in Havana seized the U.S. merchant ship *Black Warrior*, impounded its cargo of cotton bales, and jailed its captain. They further demanded that the captain pay import fees on his cargo— which was consigned to New York City—even though in eighteen previous stops at the port he had never had to pay import fees. He had stopped in Havana solely to pick up passengers, not to unload cargo. American officials in Havana protested the unlawful action to no avail; the reaction in the American press was outrage.

In response, Pierce and Marcy pressed Soulé to demand an indemnity of $300,000 from Spain to compensate the ship's owners for the detention of their ship and the loss of its cargo. The Spanish stonewalled. To gain the captain's release, the ship's owners were forced to pay a fine of $6,000. On March 15, 1854, Pierce sent a message regarding the *Black Warrior* incident to the House of Representatives. "There have been in the course of a few years past," wrote Pierce, "many other instances of aggression upon our commerce, violations of the rights of American citizens, and insults to the national flag by Spanish authorities in Cuba," yet all attempts "to obtain redress" from Spain had failed. "The offending party is at our door with large powers for aggression, yet none, it is alleged, for reparation." Cuba's "proximity" to the United States and its lengthy series of assaults on American honor threatened "peaceful relations" with Spain. "I shall not hesitate to use the authority and means which Congress may grant to insure the observance of our just rights, to obtain redress for injuries received, and to vindicate the honor of our flag."

Continuing to evoke a distinctly warlike tone, Pierce then asked the House to appropriate funds that would be available after Congress recessed should "exigency" demand their use. Pierce named no figure, but in the summer the Senate proposed $10 million—a figure, some newspapers speculated, that could fund a naval invasion of Cuba. It also appeared as though the administration was prepared to allow a massive filibustering expedition, commanded by former Mississippi governor John A. Quitman, to set sail for Cuba from New Orleans. Filibusters had in fact expected lenient treatment from Pierce, but Pierce dissolved that impression with a public proclamation in May ordering the gang Quitman had recruited to disperse and federal civilian and military personnel in New Orleans to prevent his ships from leaving port.

In June Marcy directed Soulé to drop the *Black Warrior* affair because it was clear the Spanish government would not offer compensation. Instead, he was to open discussions with that government about the purchase of Cuba from Spain by the United States up to a sales price of $130 million. Pierce, Marcy, and the U.S. ministers in Europe had learned that the Spanish government was nearly bankrupt. They knew from the former Rothschild agent August Belmont, who had intimate connections with the banking houses that held Spain's bonds, that a consortium of banks was threatening to foreclose on that country's worthless debt. Now was the moment to induce Spain to sell the island. But from Paris, John Y. Mason vigorously protested this proposal to cooperate with the banking houses and persuaded Marcy to drop it.

In frustration, Pierce thought of sending a special commission to Spain to help Soulé with the negotiations, but Congress adjourned in August 1854 without appropriating money to fund such a commission or the $10 million contingency fund Pierce had asked for. Then, fate stepped in. Daniel Sickles, whom Buchanan had sent to the United States after he had stirred outrage by refusing to stand for a toast to the queen at a public ceremony, arrived in Washington a few days after Congress adjourned. Pierce invited Sickles to the White House to discuss an alternative plan for acquiring Cuba that Pierce had hatched. Pierce wanted Buchanan, Mason, and Soulé to meet together, possibly in Paris, to devise a strategy for acquiring Cuba. He dispatched Sickles back to Europe with personal instructions to be delivered by hand to Buchanan, Mason, and Soulé, in that order.

Soulé had fled Spain after publicly encouraging rebels to overthrow the existing Spanish government in the summer of

1854—an attempt that failed. Sickles found Soulé in a small town in the French Pyrenees where he had taken refuge. By then, Soulé was so infamous for his duel and revolutionary talk that the French authorities and press kept close tabs on him. Thus the arrival of Sickles, still the secretary of the American legation in London, alerted Europeans that something was up. Nor did it help that Sickles insisted on accompanying Soulé to Paris for the proposed meeting of the American ministers; the attention to the Americans' movements intensified further. Even worse, when Soulé and Sickles arrived in the French capital to await the arrival of Buchanan from London, they found George Sanders urging Frenchmen to renew the revolution of 1848. Buchanan understood immediately that a conference among three American ministers in Paris would now be a certain public relations disaster.

Buchanan insisted that some other place be found that would afford the ministers some privacy. They eventually settled on the small town of Ostend, Belgium. Incredibly, both Sanders and Sickles accompanied Soulé and Mason on the journey and insisted on participating in the meeting. Here, Buchanan put his foot down and ordered the rabid Young America advocates to keep some distance from the ministers' deliberations. Their fellow traveler Soulé, however, informed them of the gist of the ministers' discussions.

· · ·

As Pierce's most thorough modern biographer and most determined defender, Peter A. Wallner, points out, the ministers' discussions were not meant to form a public edict about the administration's policy toward Spain and Cuba. Rather their goal was a report for the consumption of Secretary of State Marcy—an internal position paper. It stressed the dangers to the United States should Cuba's slaves be emancipated. It praised Pierce for enforcing American neutrality laws against planned filibuster expeditions against Cuba. And it predicted that if resident Cubans themselves revolted against Spain, "no human power could prevent citizens of the United States and liberal minded men of other countries from rushing to their assistance." Signed by the three ministers on October 15, 1854, and arriving in Washington on November 4, the so-called Ostend Manifesto offered no new ideas about American policy toward Spain or Cuba, as Buchanan had predicted as soon as he was ordered to the meeting.

But the ministers had posed two interesting questions: What did the refusal of Spain to sell Cuba to the United States mean? More important, was Cuba under the control of Spain a threat to the internal peace of the United States? In response to the latter question, this internal State Department document offered the sentences that would make it notorious. "Should this question be answered in the affirmative [that is, that continued Spanish control of Cuba was a threat to the United States], then by every law, human and divine, we shall be justified in wresting it from Spain, if we possess the power; and this upon the very same principle that would justify an individual in tearing down the burning house of his neighbor, if there were no other means of preventing the flames from destroying his own home." In an effort to soften this seemingly bellicose language, the report opined, "We forbear to enter into the question whether the present condition of the island would justify such a measure."

The Ostend Manifesto, in short, did not call for military seizure of Cuba if the Spanish refused to sell it. Its recommendation was far more nuanced. Nor did Pierce and Marcy, who were sorely disappointed by the lack of fresh thinking in the document, pay it much mind. They largely ignored it. Indeed, Marcy instructed Soulé after he had received the report that

Pierce opposed any action that would interfere with the peaceful relations between Spain and the United States, that Soulé was to restart negotiations for the sale of Cuba, and that if Spanish authorities continued to rebuff the offer he should cease and desist to preserve American honor. Avoiding the appearance of diplomatic groveling was an even higher priority for Pierce than the purchase of Cuba.

Soon enough, a new Spanish government, installed in late 1854 and as royalist as its predecessor, would recall the military governor who had ordered the seizure of the *Black Warrior* and make noises that it would recant the plan to free Cuba's slaves. Marcy and Pierce trusted that the Ostend report would remain one of the hundreds of such recommendations in the State Department files that would never see the light of day. Word of the document leaked to the public in 1855, however. The opposition press instantly denounced it as an outrageous highwayman's plea to seize Cuba by force for the benefit of southern slaveholders. By then the Pierce administration was an easy target. It had suffered severe, indeed almost unprecedented, political reversals during the 1854 midterm congressional elections. Pierce's foreign policy had not triggered the Democrats' losses. Rather Pierce and his party were suffering from public reaction to the president's dream of balancing Democratic sectional interests through the distribution of government jobs and a reading of the Compromise of 1850 that overturned the line demarcating slave territory from free territory that had been set by the Missouri Compromise a generation earlier.

4

Patronage, Policy, and Political Realignment

As early as December 1853, the Democratic *New York Herald*, which had strongly advocated Pierce's election in 1852 because of his commitment to the Union and the Compromise of 1850, accused Pierce of betraying that commitment. The criticism would trail Pierce for the remainder of his presidency. As proof of his supposed betrayal, the *Herald* pointed to Pierce's calamitous distribution of federal patronage positions. Rather than relying on the solid men in the center of the party who had stood by the compromise from the start, the paper's editors carped, Pierce had favored former Free Soilers from the North and disunionist Southern Rights Democrats with the juiciest plums.

The *Herald's* analysis and that of other newspapers were unfair. In the spring of 1853, Caleb Cushing dispatched a public warning to Democrats in Massachusetts, quickly labeled the *Cushing ukase*, that the administration would appoint no Democrat from the Bay State who continued to truck with Free Soilers in what was called the *Coalition*. Nevertheless, what caught the public attention of the press and the private attention of politicians between Pierce's inauguration in March and the assembling of the Thirty-third Congress in December 1853 was the administration's partiality for sectional extremes rather than the unionist center of the party. As the shrewd Georgian Alexander H. Stephens, no longer a Whig but not yet a Democrat, wrote in April 1853, Pierce "is for uniting and cementing the extreme wings of his party, the Free Soilers of the North and the Fire Eaters of the South. This is a great error."

In hindsight, it is clear that Pierce's attempts to distribute the loaves and fishes among all elements of the party proved an unmitigated disaster. Politicians who considered themselves worthy of selection fumed when members of rival factions instead got the jobs. Some of this anger had nothing to do with the administration's commitment to the compromise. In Pennsylvania, for example, the German-born newspaper editor Francis Grund, who was aligned with Simon Cameron's rather than Buchanan's faction of the state Democratic Party, declared open war on the administration after the appointment of James Campbell, a Catholic, as postmaster general. Stephen Douglas's supporters in the Midwest railed that Robert McClelland was giving the best positions in the Interior Department to Lewis Cass's friends. In almost every state of the Union, the allotment of federal jobs created controversy and outrage.

The apparent favoritism had important political ramifications. Incumbent and newly elected Democratic senators and representatives from the South, almost all of whom formerly belonged to the anti-compromise wing of the party, deeply deplored the widely, if erroneously, reported preference shown by Pierce for antislavery Democrats in the North. During 1853, therefore, they began to contemplate ways to enforce a prosouthern Democratic orthodoxy on those antislavery appointees as the price of their confirmation by the Senate.

On the other hand, the minority of pro-compromise Democrats from the South, especially those who had joined Union parties in Georgia, Alabama, and Mississippi in 1850 and 1851, were deeply incensed by the administration's preference for their Southern Rights rivals, a preference vividly demarcated by Jefferson Davis's elevation to the War Department and Pierre Soulé's appointment to Spain. By the summer and fall of 1853, southern newspapers reported that these men were contemplating rejoining Whigs and forming a newly constituted Union Party. Preserving the unity of the Democratic coalition that had elected Pierce required averting that threat.

The opposition among pro-compromise southern Democrats to Pierce's patronage allocation in 1853 was so overt and widespread that southern members of former president Millard Fillmore's cabinet, notably Alexander H. H. Stuart of Virginia and John Pendleton Kennedy of Maryland, insisted to Fillmore throughout 1853 that those Democrats could be recruited to a new Union Party that might elect Fillmore president in 1856. Fillmore, who had long been on the outs with the antislavery and anti-compromise majority wing of the New York Whig Party, considered such a partisan reorganization both possible and desirable. Yet he and his former cabinet members realistically understood that any such attempt to organize a new party hinged on a third key group, Democrats in the North—and especially in New York—who had supported the compromise before it had even passed. The fury with which those Democrats, known in New York as Hard-Shells, greeted Pierce's patronage policy seemed to offer an opening to conservative Whig enthusiasts for a new Union Party.

If newspaper coverage is any indication, nothing regarding politics in 1853 captured public attention so much as the intraparty brawl over patronage allocation in New York State. By that year, there were three discernible factions in the state's Democratic Party. The Barnburners, who had supported Van Buren's candidacy in 1848 and who constituted a clear majority of the party, were now led by John A. Dix. The Soft-Shell

Hunkers, who had supported Cass in 1848 and had welcomed the Barnburners back to the Democratic fold in 1849, were led by William L. Marcy, whom Pierce had named to the top post in his cabinet. Finally, the Hard-Shell Hunkers were led by former senator Daniel S. Dickinson and insisted that Barnburner rebels be denied any elective or appointive office. Dickinson arguably stands as one of the most important if now forgotten politicians of the antebellum period.

Pierce's response to this tripartite rift was to divide the hundreds of federal jobs in New York as equally as possible among the factions. Having elevated Marcy to the cabinet, he appointed Dix as subtreasurer in New York City, a stopgap, he vainly hoped, until he could name Dix as minister to France. But Pierce reserved for the Hard-Shell wing what was by any measure the prime patronage job available to the U.S. government: customs collector in New York City. Through fees exacted on importing merchants, the collector could earn tens of thousands of dollars above his regular salary. He could also appoint subordinate customs officials not simply in the city's harbor but also in towns along the Hudson River up to Albany. Altogether, historians estimate, the holder of this post could hire between one and two thousand men who could be the basis for a powerful political machine capable of controlling the party's nominating conventions.

To balance his allotment of New York's jobs, Pierce offered the collectorship to Dickinson, but with a caveat. The subordinate jobs at the collector's disposal, Pierce insisted, must be divided evenly among the three Democratic factions. Irked by that requirement, Dickinson spurned the job. Another Hard-Shell Democrat, a man named Greene C. Bronson, was found who would take it, yet subsequently he made no attempt to distribute the subordinate positions evenly and instead gave the lion's share to his allies. By October 1853 he was engaged in a widely publicized spat with Treasury Secretary Guthrie. In a public letter Guthrie rebuked Bronson for flouting administration policy; in a public letter of reply Bronson denied that he had ever signed any pledge to heed it and that all of the men he had appointed were loyal Democrats who supported the national platform's pledge to the Union and the Compromise of 1850. Their exchange was reprinted in Democratic and Whig newspapers as far away from New York as Georgia, Mississippi, Iowa, and Wisconsin.

In the meantime, at Dickinson's command, Hards refused to attend the regular state Democratic nominating convention, spurning the Barnburners and Soft-Shell Democrats to establish their own slate of state officers for the election campaigns in 1853. As a result of this split, New York was one of only two northern states where Whigs triumphed that year. In retaliation for the Hards' bolt, after the election Pierce ordered Guthrie to fire Bronson. To avenge that move, Hards vowed to find some way to deny the Senate confirmation of Pierce's Barnburner and Soft appointees. In this regard, the southern Democrats, also infuriated by Pierce's appointment of antislavery Democrats, appeared to be natural allies.

By the fall of 1853, many Democrats worried that their party was approaching internal disintegration, just as Whigs and Democrats alike had predicted after the Democrats' overwhelming victories in 1852. In July the U.S. marshal from the western district of Pennsylvania had warned Caleb Cushing that the state's Democrats were in total disarray and that the best way to reunite them was for Pierce to initiate some policy "that will raise invective from the other side and compel us to quit our domestic squabbles." Similarly, as Congress opened in December, a Missouri Democrat wrote Illinois senator Stephen Douglas that unless Pierce "promptly marks out a line of sound national and Democratic policy, and makes it known to the country by unmistakable *action*, it will be impossible for him to save his Administration from total Failure." Nothing but the "boldest and most determined action can turn the current" and prevent the Democratic Party from being "shivered to atoms."

Douglas took that warning to heart. Pierce seemed oblivious to the problem. His first annual message to Congress that December contained only one significant request that concerned domestic policy. Congress, he advised, should lower the already very low Walker Tariff of 1846, a request the overwhelming Democratic majorities in the House and Senate ignored. One line in the prolix message, however, bears quotation because of its unintended irony. Alluding to the relaxation of sectional tensions brought on by the Compromise of 1850, Pierce avowed: "That this repose is to suffer no shock during my official term, if I have the power to avert it, those who placed me here may be assured." Moreover, Pierce seemed to go out of his way to put the kibosh on other domestic policies that might reinspirit Democratic Party loyalty. He noted the great popular interest in building a transcontinental railroad to the Pacific coast—after all, that was the purpose of the Gadsden Purchase—but then indicated that it would be unconstitutional for Congress to provide any federal subsidies for its construction. Put differently, the opportunity for some other Democrat to frame a "Democratic policy" that might "raise invective from the other [that is, Whig] side" fell to other men, and Douglas seized it.

· · ·

Press reaction to Pierce's first annual message was, predictably, mixed. Most Democratic papers praised it, but the hostile Whig *Boston Atlas* dismissed it "as the weakest, most inane and unsatisfactory document, that ever emanated from the head of the nation." More important was the reaction of the widely read Democratic *New York Herald*. Like Whig papers, the *Herald* criticized the vagueness of the message, its reliance on strained rhetorical flourishes to gloss over the absence of a specific blueprint that made clear what the administration hoped to do. The *Herald*'s editors also faulted Pierce for what he had omitted entirely from the address. Of those omissions named in the editorial, the most significant was Pierce's utter silence on the subject of Nebraska.

Nebraska referred to the still unorganized area of the Louisiana Purchase Territory west of Missouri, Iowa, and Minnesota Territory. By the early 1850s pressure was growing from two different northern groups to formally organize the area. One was farmers seeking cheaper land than could be found in burgeoning midwestern states. Those farmers could not gain legal title to any land in the Louisiana Territory until Congress established formal territorial governments. Only then could the federal government survey the land and put it up for sale at government offices. Since the acquisition of Oregon and California, moreover, numerous proposals had sprung up to build one or more railroads to the Pacific coast. What route or routes such railroads might take generated considerable dispute, but almost everyone, save the rigid strict constructionist Pierce, recognized that this ambitious project required federal land grants, which the railroads could sell to raise construction funds. Any route from the Midwest across the Louisiana Territory, however, required the government to survey land into sections that could be granted to railroad companies. Proponents of a transcontinental railroad thus joined land-hungry farmers in pressing for the formal territorial organization of the area west of Missouri and Iowa. By the end of 1853, territorial organization for Nebraska had emerged on the front burner of congressional business. Within days of the opening of the Thirty-fourth

Congress in December, a Democratic senator from Iowa introduced a bill to do just that.

Southern and Hard-Shell critics of Pierce's patronage policies would seize upon the Nebraska question to challenge the Senate confirmation of Pierce's antislavery appointees. Douglas hoped the Nebraska issue might help reignite interparty combat between Democrats and Whigs and thus restore his own party's internal cohesion. Nebraska was also the issue that helped wreck the Pierce administration politically and propel not simply a major voter realignment in the North against the Democratic Party but, even more important in the long run, a reorganization of the political opposition against Pierce's Democratic Party. One of the new parties that emerged in reaction to the organization of Nebraska, which Pierce endorsed, was the Republican Party, and it was the victory of that party in the presidential election of 1860 that provoked secession and the Civil War. Historians almost uniformly rank Pierce among the nation's worst presidents, indeed, because of his role in securing organization of Nebraska and thus bringing on the Civil War.

What made the Nebraska question so potentially explosive was slavery. All of the area in any proposed territory that would be carved out lay north of the latitude line thirty-six degrees, thirty minutes, from which slavery had been "forever prohibited" by the Missouri Compromise of 1820. Even before December 1853, southern Democrats had made it clear that they would allow no territorial organization on those terms. Slaveholders in Missouri, who were particularly numerous near the state's western boundary, feared that any new free territory on their border would become a refuge for their absconding slaves. Other slave-state Democrats, having denounced the Wilmot Proviso as an insult to southern honor and a violation of southern equality since 1846, now found the prohibition in the act of 1820 intolerable. What is more, still grousing about the 1850 admission of California as a free state that upset the sectional balance in the Senate, they began to pay heed to Democratic slaveholders from western Missouri, especially Senator David R. Atchison, who argued that slavery could be just as profitable on the western as the eastern bank of the Missouri River. Here, then, was a long-shot chance to add a new slave state to the Union, but that chance depended on finessing, if not outright repealing, the ban on slavery in the Missouri Compromise.

Douglas, as chairman of the Senate committee on territories that had jurisdiction over the newly introduced Nebraska bill, had sought the formal organization of the area since he first entered the House of Representatives in 1844. A strong nationalist, he hoped to develop the West as a balance wheel between the North and South. He was also just as firmly committed to preserving the internal unity of the Democratic Party as was Pierce, and he took quite seriously the warnings of Democratic disintegration unless the party developed some specific program that provoked opposition from the few remaining Whigs in Congress. Because Whigs had traditionally opposed western development, he shaped a program of western development that might do the trick. He called for the formal organization of Nebraska Territory, the chartering of a transcontinental railroad across that territory, and a new homestead law to attract settlers to the area. Douglas explicitly advised his allies that his three-part program "will form the Test of parties."

The linchpin of the program was Nebraska, and by the end of 1853 Douglas knew that would prove impossible unless he could find some way around the Missouri Compromise's slavery prohibition. Yet he also recognized that an outright repeal of that ban would spawn outrage in the North. Thus Douglas was attracted to suggestions that had appeared in some Democratic newspapers during 1853—namely, to apply the popular sovereignty provisions of the Utah and New Mexico territorial legislation of 1850 to the Nebraska bill.

The first version of the legislation Douglas introduced to the Senate on January 4, 1854, copied word-for-word the provisions from the Utah and New Mexico acts specifying that any states formed from the territory should be admitted to the Union with or without slavery as their own constitutions prescribed at the time. Douglas accompanied this version of the bill with a report that explicitly counseled against either reaffirming or repealing the Missouri Compromise's prohibition of slavery. Then and later, Douglas offered the spurious rationale that in 1850 Congress had extended popular sovereignty over all territories, not just Utah and New Mexico. No explicit evidence exists, but Douglas may have hoped that this invocation of the Compromise of 1850 might keep pro-compromise southern Democrats in the party fold—and out of a revived Union Party that some Whigs hoped to build.

In any event, this version did not satisfy the anti-compromise southern Democrats whose votes Douglas needed, even though it clearly nullified any eternal prohibition of slavery. They complained that under Douglas's bill, the 1820 prohibition might still apply during Nebraska's entire territorial stage, keeping slaveholders out of it and ensuring that the new state constitutions would be antislavery as a result. They insisted that he rework the bill to give slaveholders a greater chance of access to the territory.

On January 10, Douglas offered a revised version stating that the territorial legislature could make the decision whether to allow or prohibit slavery in Nebraska. The New York Whig William H. Seward believed that this was as far toward outright repeal of the ban as Douglas dared to go, and he attributed the change to pressure from New York's Hards, who wanted a new standard of party orthodoxy to which antislavery Democratic appointees dared not subscribe. Hard-Shell Hunkers were in fact jubilant. "I am . . . glad," one wrote Douglas, "that there is now a measure before Congress that will test the sincerity of the late Free Soil Democrats whom Gen. Pierce has taken to his bosom." "The Hards or Dickinsonites . . . are exulting," a New York Soft told Marcy in February. "They say that they have at last cornered the President with the Nebraska bill."

If Hards were pleased with the claim that the legislation of 1850 had wiped out the Missouri prohibition, a few southerners thought this version flawed because the 1820 ban might still apply until a territorial legislature was elected, meaning that no proslavery men would sit in it. Two men were most important here. In the House, Alabama Democrat Philip Phillips called for outright repeal of the ban. On January 16 in the Senate, Kentucky Whig Archibald Dixon promised that when the Senate's agenda allowed it, he would offer an amendment to Douglas's bill flatly repealing the ban. Refusing to be out-flanked by their southern Whig opponents on the slavery question, southern Democratic senators renewed pressure on Douglas to change the bill. He did so by adding explicit language that the Compromise of 1850 had rendered the 1820 prohibition inoperative. He recognized that this change would be so offensive to many northerners, including northern Democrats, that he decided to seek Pierce's personal support for the measure to bring administration pressure on northern Democratic congressmen. Through the auspices of Secretary of War Jefferson Davis, a meeting was arranged with Pierce at the White House on Sunday, January 22, even though Pierce was loath to conduct any official business on the Sabbath.

Attending this meeting along with Davis, Pierce, and Douglas were Philip Phillips; John C. Breckinridge, a Democratic congressman from Kentucky who had emerged as the administration's floor leader in the House; and the four most powerful southern Democrats in the Senate, who roomed in the same boardinghouse and were thus known as the F-Street Mess: David R. Atchison of Missouri, James M. Mason and Robert M. T. Hunter of Virginia, and Andrew Pickens Butler of South Carolina. Our knowledge of what was said during this two-hour meeting depends exclusively on memoirs written long after the fact. Phillips later recalled, for example, that after scanning the proposed bill, Pierce said, "Gentlemen, you are entering a serious undertaking, and the ground should be well surveyed before the first step is taken." Pierce and his cabinet had in fact been following developments in the Senate closely, and the preceding day they had agreed that the kind of overt repeal demanded by Phillips and Dixon would ruin the Democratic Party in the North, where mass protest meetings against Douglas's measure were already gathering.

Whatever arguments were used to persuade Pierce to go along with the bill, they succeeded. Indeed, Pierce insisted on personally writing down its crucial language. The Missouri Compromise, penned Pierce, had been "superceded by the principles of the legislation of 1850, commonly called the compromise measures and is hereby declared inoperative and void." The residents of any territory, he concluded, "were perfectly free to form and regulate their institutions in their own way." This was the version of the bill that Douglas presented to the Senate the following day, with one significant revision. Now two territories—Kansas, west of Missouri, and Nebraska, west of Iowa and running north to the Canadian border—were to be organized. This change created the impression that a deal had been cut: Kansas would be slave; Nebraska would be free. Douglas would make one other critical change in the bill a few days later. Now the principle of the 1850 compromise that had supposedly obviated the Missouri Compromise ban was specified as congressional nonintervention in the decision about slavery, rather than the right of people in territorial legislatures to make it, a formulation far more pleasing to southerners.

. . .

Signing off on the Kansas-Nebraska bill, which the administration's newspaper in Washington quickly made clear was now a measure that all loyal Democrats were expected to support, was the biggest mistake of Franklin Pierce's political career. Why, numerous historians have asked, did he do it? One reason most likely concerned the foreign policy on which Pierce believed the historical reputation of his presidency would rest. Gadsden's treaty and the still uncompleted reciprocity treaty with Canada required Senate ratification, and the four members of the F-Street Mess who were pressing him to go along with the Nebraska bill had the power to deep-six those treaties should he buck them. James M. Mason, after all, chaired the Senate's foreign relations committee.

Alternatively, some historians point to Pierce's allegedly craven disposition to seek southern approval. Douglas and Pierce himself were the only northern Democrats at that Sunday meeting, and they were outnumbered by seven strong-willed southerners. Yet Pierce was not a weak man or easily intimidated. Nor, given his strong efforts to stop filibustering expeditions against Cuba that many southerners favored, did he always seek to please southerners.

A more likely possibility is that Douglas persuaded Pierce of the validity of the case he was already making in the Senate— namely, that the territorial provisions of the Compromise of 1850, to which the party's 1852 platform was pledged, had been meant to apply to all territories, not just Utah and New Mexico. That was the rationale he used in the language he set out himself and he would state it again in a private letter in the summer of 1854.

Finally, Pierce's most recent biographer argues that Pierce was motivated by his obsession with preserving the internal unity of the Democratic Party. According to this interpretation, had he refused to endorse the measure or—more dramatically— threatened to veto it should it reach his desk, he risked an almost certain breach with the most powerful members of the congressional wing of his own party. Pierce certainly had grounds for taking either course. Not only did the Democratic national platform of 1852 commit the party to upholding the compromise; it also pledged that the party would never again allow a matter involving slavery to come before Congress, a pledge Pierce had reiterated in his recent annual message. Yet, according to this view, preserving comity with congressional Democrats, rather than adhering to the party platform, was Pierce's top priority.

My own guess is a variation on this theme. We simply do not know what was said at that meeting. But it seems likely to me that one of the arguments Douglas made reflected the warning he received in December. The Democratic Party would be "shivered to atoms" by internecine quarrels over patronage unless the Democrats developed some program that provoked opposition from the Whigs. Caleb Cushing, Pierce's most influential cabinet adviser, had received a similar warning in July 1853, one he most likely passed on to the president. Nothing that Pierce had asked Congress to do in his annual message had the potential of spurring the united Whig opposition, a development that seemed necessary to bring warring Democrats back together. Douglas's Nebraska bill most certainly did. Reuniting Democrats in the states who were at loggerheads over Pierce's misguided patronage policies, even more than preserving Democratic unity in Washington, may explain the president's decision.

One other factor probably contributed to it: overconfidence about northern Democrats' ability to win the upcoming mid-term congressional elections by defending congressional noninterference. Recall Pierce's letter of 1852, meant for distribution at the Democratic national convention, in which he touted New Hampshire Democrats' ability to win elections while defending the Fugitive Slave Act. In August 1854 he privately wrote to a New Yorker that Democrats had won in 1852 by defending the principles of the Compromise of 1850. He insisted that they could do so again in 1854 if they would only come out openly in favor of those principles against Whig criticism of the Nebraska measure. Yet the North was not New Hampshire—or at least not the New Hampshire of 1851 and 1852 writ large—as Pierce already had reason to know by then. Like Douglas, Pierce apparently envisioned that the major battle over the Kansas-Nebraska bill would be with the traditional Whig foe, whose electoral weakness had been demonstrated in 1852 and 1853.

When Douglas presented the latest version of his bill to the Senate on January 23, 1854, in fact, the chances that all Whigs, southerners as well as northerners, would oppose it were quite good. What evidence we have about popular or at least Whig newspaper opinion in the South suggests profound disbelief that slavery might actually take hold in Kansas and considerable fury that Democrats, by betraying their 1852 platform pledge, were inviting a renewal of sectional conflict over slavery expansion. Northern conservative pro-compromise Whigs fully agreed with that analysis, while northern antislavery Whigs, led by New York's William Seward, were certain to oppose the bill because it opened up to potential settlement by slaveholders an area from which slavery had been prohibited for thirty-four years. A partisan, rather than a sectional, battle over the Nebraska bill, in short, appeared likely. The Whig minority seemed certain to lose that battle in Congress, but the congressional and state elections slated for 1854 and 1855 seemed a very different matter.

The menace of Whig unity against Douglas's measure evaporated the day after he presented it. On Tuesday, January 24, 1854, the few remaining Free Soil members of Congress published "The Appeal of Independent Democrats in Congress to the People of the United States" in the Washington *National Era*, the main organ of their party. This manifesto, one of the most masterful pieces of political propaganda written in the nineteenth century, arraigned Douglas's bill as a "gross violation of a sacred pledge," as "part and parcel of an atrocious plot" to spread slavery and exclude northern whites from the new territories, and as a "bold scheme against American liberty" that would subjugate the entire nation "to the yoke of a slaveholding despotism." This charge changed everything, for it preempted the grounds for Whig opposition to the bill. From a bisectional Whig condemnation of a measure that threatened sectional peace, opposition shifted to a bitter sectional complaint about aggression by the southern Slave Power against the North. By identifying opposition to the measure with men most southerners regarded as abolitionists, it also made it impossible for most southern Whigs to oppose the measure in Congress. "It is unfortunate that the free soil senators have been suffered to lead off the opposition," complained one of Millard Fillmore's conservative Whig allies in Congress. "This fact more than anything else has contributed to unite southern opinion on the bill."

Indeed, it had. Free Soil characterizations of the bill as an act of aggression against the North forced southern Whigs to support it just as they had joined southern Democrats in opposition to the Wilmot Proviso. In the Senate, where the bill passed easily in March, nine of eleven southern Whigs supported passage and only two opposed it. In the House, where the bill passed much more narrowly in May by a vote of 113 to 100, thirteen southern Whigs provided the necessary winning margin; only seven southern Whigs voted nay, and four abstained. Had southern Whigs united in opposition to the bill, it would have gone down to defeat. Their thirteen votes were necessary, in turn, only because Pierce's hope of uniting the Democratic Party behind the Kansas-Nebraska bill proved a dismal failure. Northern Democrats in the House of Representatives who voted on the measure in May split 44 in favor and 43 against. A healthy respect for public opinion in their districts that overwhelmingly opposed opening the territory to settlement by slaveholders explains those votes. That the Kansas-Nebraska bill had passed with support from southern Whigs infuriated northern Whigs, who complained that this had permanently "denationalized" their own party. Pierce signed the bill into law at the end of May 1854, the second biggest mistake of his political career.

On the very night that the House passed the bill, a fugitive slave named Anthony Burns was captured in Boston. A few nights later, a mob aroused by speeches at an abolitionist rally tried to storm the courthouse where he was held in a vain attempt to free him. What they managed instead was to kill a deputy U.S. marshal stationed to guard the courthouse. Boston's mayor called out the state militia, and the marshal asked Pierce for and received permission to bring in units of federal troops to help remand Burns to his Virginia owners. With that show of military muscle, Burns was loaded on a ship heading for Virginia without incident, but the Burns episode helped fix Pierce's reputation as a proslavery doughface in Boston. The rest of the North, however, was far more concerned about the implications of the Nebraska measure.

"I think a mistake has been made in this Nebraska business," wailed a New York Democrat after Pierce signed the law. "The effect will be to consolidate the Whig party in the North &

divide the Democrats." The refusal of northern Democrats to give the measure unanimous support became clear even before it was enacted. To Pierce's deep chagrin, in late January the New Hampshire Democratic state convention refused even to mention the bill that had been declared administration policy. Later that year, Democratic conventions in New York, Pennsylvania, and other states pursued the same tack. Silence, however, provided no political safety from the North's wrathful electorate. In the fall elections of 1854, Democrats suffered crushing defeats in the North, in part because tens of thousands of former Democratic voters bolted to the opposition while thousands of others expressed their dismay by shunning the polls altogether. Incumbent Democratic governors met defeat in New York, Pennsylvania, Iowa, and Michigan. Democrats lost sixty-six of the ninety-one northern congressional seats they held. Only seven of the forty-four representatives who voted for the Nebraska bill won reelection. The results in some states were simply astonishing. Maine, Michigan, and Indiana were traditionally Democratic states, yet Democrats carried only one of Maine's six congressional seats, one of Michigan's four, and two of Indiana's eleven. More striking still, Democrats won only five of New York's thirty-three seats; they lost all of Ohio's twenty-one districts; and they were shut out in Massachusetts as well. The rout continued in the spring elections of 1855. Democrats lost every congressional seat in Connecticut, Rhode Island, and, most strikingly, Pierce's own New Hampshire. Pierce had helped to end Democratic dominance in his home state.

· · ·

If the 1854 and 1855 elections witnessed a massive repudiation of Franklin Pierce's party and the policy he had foolishly endorsed, it was not instantly clear who had benefited most from that rebuff. Northern voters had begun a marked realignment against Pierce's party, but it did not necessarily benefit that party's traditional foe, the Whigs. Instead, a diverse conglomeration of new political coalitions emerged to compete with the Whigs for the anti-Democratic vote. Within two years these newcomers would send the venerable Whig Party to its grave.

A crucial facet of nineteenth-century political life can help the modern reader understand how this could happen. After all, today's major parties, the Democrats and Republicans, appear almost invulnerable to challenges from new parties. But that invulnerability is largely attributable to the fact that state governments print the ballots voters cast, punch, or mark, and the same governments control the access that parties have to those publicly printed ballots. Thus challengers to the major parties must jump through hoops, usually by collecting signatures on petitions, to get on the ballot so that people might have a chance to vote for them. In the nineteenth century, however, governments did not print and distribute ballots. That was the job of the political parties themselves. In effect, this system meant that all that was needed to launch a new party was access to printing presses and enough volunteer manpower to distribute its ballots at the polls. That was the scenario in the extraordinarily tumultuous elections of 1854–55 in which the northern electorate repudiated Pierce's party.

In the midwestern states where Whigs were least competitive by the end of 1853 and where many angry Whig politicos vowed never again to cooperate with southern Whigs because of their betrayal on Nebraska—Ohio, Indiana, Michigan, Wisconsin, and the northern third of Illinois—Whig leaders in effect posted "Gone Out of Business" signs on the doors of party headquarters. These Whigs joined anti-Nebraska Democrats and Free Soilers in fusion anti-Nebraska coalitions. In Michigan, Wisconsin, and northern counties in Illinois, these coalitions called themselves the Republican Party, and the platform adopted by the Michigan Republican state convention in the summer of 1854 ringingly declared the mission of this new party. After denouncing slavery as "a relic of barbarism," calling for renewed defiance of the Fugitive Slave Act, and insisting that Congress prohibit slavery extension to check the "unequal representation" of the South in Washington, D.C., it declared that the purpose of the Kansas-Nebraska Act was to "give the Slave States such a decided and practical preponderance in all measures of government as shall reduce the North . . . to the mere province of a few slaveholding oligarchs of the South—to a condition too shameful to be contemplated." The party's platform concluded: "That in view of the necessity of battling for the first principles of republican government, and against the schemes of aristocracy the most revolting and oppressive with which the earth was ever cursed, or man debased, we will co-operate and be known as Republicans until the contest be terminated." In short, the mission of the Republican Party was less opposition to slavery than opposition to southern slaveholders, and this would be the primary theme of Republican campaigners until the Civil War. In other midwestern states, however, the anti-Nebraska coalitions that emerged in 1854 simply called themselves the Opposition or sometimes the People's Party. The nomenclature is important, for no one knew in 1854 and 1855 that the Republican Party might emerge as the permanent opponent of the Democrats in American political life. Instead, Democrats' foes had joined in ad hoc coalitions determined to reimpose the Missouri Compromise ban on Kansas and Nebraska.

Elsewhere, northern Whigs refused to give up the fight by declaring their party moribund. After all, every northern Whig in the House and Senate had voted against the Nebraska bill, and many northern Whigs and Democrats alike believed that stance would produce northern Whig victories in 1854, 1855, and the presidential election of 1856. These Whigs welcomed support from Free Soilers and anti-Nebraska Democrats, but they insisted on running as Whigs, not as candidates of some new cobbled-together coalition. Abraham Lincoln, to take one example, spurned overtures from residents of northern Illinois to join the new Republican Party, and he ran for the state legislature in 1854 as a straight-out Whig. Iowa's Whigs, who won the governorship in 1854 for the first time since that state's admission in 1846, also insisted on retaining the Whig organization. Still, the greatest resistance to partisan reorganization in 1854 came from Whigs east of Ohio, where the Whig Party had always been strongest.

• • •

Yet those Whigs met and ultimately succumbed to a different new challenger for anti-Democratic votes. This was the anti-immigrant, anti-Catholic, and antipolitician American or Know Nothing movement, which vowed to destroy both the Democratic and Whig parties. Between 1846, the year of the Irish potato famine, and 1854, more than 3 million Irish and German immigrants, the vast majority of whom were Roman Catholics, had arrived in the United States. Southern cities such as Savannah, Mobile, New Orleans, Saint Louis, and Baltimore received some of this influx, but most immigrants headed for northern cities. To this flood of immigrants, native-born Protestants, who had been warned for decades by bigoted ministers about a papal plot to undermine the American republic, attributed a number of evils—the growth in crime, poverty, public drunkenness, and competition for jobs—to these immigrant "minions" of the pope. The competition for jobs became a particular grievance of native-born manual workers when the economy plunged into a recession during the last half of 1854.

Nonetheless, it was the increased political clout of Catholic immigrants that did the most to spur the growth of Know Nothingism in 1854 and 1855. The chief political goals of the Know Nothing movement were to bar all immigrants and all Catholics, whether native- or foreign-born, from holding public office and to increase the naturalization period for immigrants from five to twenty-one years—when, that is, the objective was not to abolish naturalization, which brought the right to vote, altogether. The election of 1852 did much to fan nativist fears. That year both the Whigs and Democrats openly courted the Catholic immigrant vote. The number of immigrants voting, almost all of them voting Democratic, soared. And in the wake of that contest, Franklin Pierce had appointed an Irish Catholic as his postmaster general in an apparently overt bid for Catholic support. In the eyes of anti-Catholic nativists, both the Democrats and the Whigs stood guilty of undermining the Protestant republic.

What emerged as the Know Nothing movement actually began years before the 1852 election. In 1849 an anti-immigrant, anti-Catholic fanatic named Charles B. Allen had tried to start a secret, superpatriotic fraternity known as the Order of the Star Spangled Banner. As of mid-1852 it had a grand membership of nine men meeting in a back alley in New York City. Then it was taken over by another nativist group known as the Order of United Americans, led by a superb organizer named James W. Barker. By the end of 1854 the membership of the order totaled somewhere between eight hundred thousand and 1.5 million men, most of them skilled, semiskilled, and unskilled laborers or lower-middle-class white-collar clerks, who were sworn by membership oaths to support the political candidates endorsed by the local lodges or wigwams of the order. Membership was supposed to remain absolutely secret, and the sobriquet "Know Nothing" came from members' professing to know nothing about the order when questioned by outsiders. At first, the Know Nothings endorsed candidates of the major parties. But then they began to nominate their own candidates, and in the fall of 1853 and spring local elections of 1854 they startled outsiders by electing men no one else knew were even seeking office. The order's most rapid growth and the most vivid demonstration of its political power, however, coincided with the furious northern reaction to the passage of the Kansas-Nebraska Act in the summer and fall of 1854.

That coincidence has caused one historian, Tyler Anbinder, to attribute the growth of northern Know Nothingism to anti-Nebraska sentiment, rather than to anti-immigrant, anti-Catholic, and anti-political-incumbent sentiment. This argument has three flaws. First, Know Nothingism mushroomed in the South, especially in southern cities, just as rapidly as it did in the North in late 1854, and clearly anti-Nebraska sentiment had nothing to do with that growth. Second, the authenticity of the anti-Catholic and anti-immigrant sentiment powering the movement in the North and in cities like Baltimore, Louisville, Saint Louis, and New Orleans is simply overwhelming. After observing a Know Nothing sweep of Cincinnati's October 1854 elections, for example, the young Whig and future Republican president Rutherford B. Hayes exclaimed in his diary, "How people do hate Catholics, and what happiness it was to thousands to have a chance to show it in what seemed like a lawful and patriotic manner" by voting Know Nothing. Third, and most important, Know Nothing candidates often defeated Whigs running on an anti-Nebraska platform in various northern states in 1854. When Whigs won that year, it was usually because Know

Nothings had backed them, and when anti-Nebraska Whig candidates lacked that backing they often lost.

In sum, the hatred of Catholics and immigrants that the Know Nothings harnessed in 1854 and 1855 had as much to do with the rout of Democrats in those years as did anger at the Kansas-Nebraska Act. All of the congressmen elected in Massachusetts in November 1854 and in New England in March and April 1855 were Know Nothings, as were scores of Whig or Opposition congressmen elected in 1854 in New York, New Jersey, Pennsylvania, Ohio, Indiana, and Michigan. The northern Whig Party was done in not by anti-Nebraska sentiment, which northern Whigs hoped to exploit, but by Know Nothingism, which was determined to destroy the Whig Party because it had openly solicited Catholic immigrant support in 1852. Only after the inroads of the Know Nothings into the Whigs' northern electoral base had been made plain by the 1854 election results did such men as William Seward and Abraham Lincoln give up on their cherished Whig Party and decide to throw their support to the new Republican Party.

But tens of thousands of Democrats also joined the new Know Nothing Party, and not simply in the North. In 1855 slave-state voters sent twenty-five more Know Nothings to Congress. Because Know Nothings had strength in both the North and South, quite unlike the new, exclusively northern, Republican Party, many people predicted that Know Nothings would elect the next president in 1856. When the new Thirty-fourth Congress assembled in December 1855, it was clear that Democrats were now in a distinct minority in the House, but it was unclear whether Know Nothings or anti-Nebraska men who had been elected under a variety of labels had the majority. The upshot was that it took the badly fragmented House two full months to elect a Speaker. The final outcome of that contest, in turn, was powerfully influenced by what happened in Kansas Territory during 1855.

. . .

It took several months after Pierce signed the Kansas-Nebraska Act on May 30, 1854, for the government's land office to survey the land in Kansas and put it up for sale. So it was only in the fall of the year that settlers began to arrive in any significant numbers and that Andrew H. Reeder of Easton, Pennsylvania, whom Pierce appointed as territorial governor upon the recommendation of Postmaster General Campbell, made his way to the new territory. Reeder turned out to be a remarkably poor choice. He was primarily interested in making a quick buck through land speculation, not in governing the territory, and he quickly alienated early settlers by trying to locate the territorial capital many miles west of where they had taken up farms. Most of those early settlers were small farmers from the Midwest and nonslaveholders from the upper South, including some Missourians. Most had little interest in the question of extending slavery and shared a desire to keep all blacks, free or slave, out of Kansas. Nonetheless, some slaveholders hoping to create a new slave state did appear in Kansas along with their chattels, as did some New Englanders whose primary goal was to stop slavery extension by controlling the new territorial government. Of vast importance, almost all northerners moving to Kansas did so by traveling up the Missouri River from Saint Louis, a route that carried them through the heart of slaveholding country in western Missouri. The Missouri slaveholders regarded these northern settlers as an invasion of abolitionists, and they redoubled their determination to legalize slavery in Kansas.

The pivotal episode was the election of the first territorial legislature, which Reeder had postponed until March 30, 1855.

Egged on by former senator David R. Atchison, whose Senate term had ended early that March, hundreds of heavily armed Missourians, aiming to exploit an ambiguity in the original act as to what constituted "residency" in Kansas, poured across the border on election day. These "Border Ruffians" took over polling places in sparsely populated hamlets and cast not only their own ballots but hundreds of additional, wholly fictitious, ballots for proslavery legislative candidates. The feckless Reeder allowed most of those results to stand. The fraud yielded a heavy majority of proslavery men in the new legislature, and upon its meeting in July 1855 they immediately passed draconian proslavery laws. To hold office in the territory, including its legislature, one had to swear an oath that slavery was and would forever remain legal in Kansas. Harboring a fugitive slave was made punishable by ten years at hard labor, and circulating abolitionist literature became a capital offense. In response to these laws, men elected by northerners angrily resigned from the new territorial legislature and helped set up a rival "free state" Kansas government in the town of Topeka, a government that the Pierce administration denounced as an outlaw regime. That summer Pierce fired Reeder because of his land speculation, but his replacement, Wilson Shannon of Ohio, proved no more ready than Reeder to persuade the legislature to recant its proslavery laws. By the end of 1855 there appeared to be a real possibility that southerners might succeed in making Kansas a new slave state. That possibility affected what happened in the House when Congress assembled in December.

So did another event during 1855. In June the first national council meeting of Know Nothings assembled in Philadelphia. Consisting of seven members from each state council of the secret fraternity, the national council would officially rename the organization the American Party and renounce secrecy.

But it also revealed that the Know Nothings were no more immune to a sectional rift over slavery extension than were the Whigs and Democrats. Virtually all northern Know Nothings shared the general outrage in their section over the Kansas-Nebraska Act, and they urged the national council to go on record in favor of a restitution of the Missouri Compromise prohibition in Kansas and Nebraska. To the northerners' dismay, southerners refused. Section Twelve of the adopted national platform in effect acquiesced in the Kansas-Nebraska Act despite what had happened in Kansas. The decision caused a minority of northern Know Nothings, most notably Senator Henry Wilson of Massachusetts, an old Free Soiler, to bolt the nativist party and join the Republicans. Other northern men, elected to Congress as Know Nothings in 1854 and early 1855, did not yet bolt, but they were determined to establish their anti-Nebraska bona fides when Congress met. Events in Kansas and Philadelphia during 1855 caused many men who had been elected as Whigs, Oppositionists, or Know Nothings in 1854 and 1855 to reconsider the possibility of enlisting behind the Republican banner when Congress convened in December.

The man who most benefited from this shift of sentiment was another Massachusetts Know Nothing, Representative Nathaniel P. Banks. Banks had been elected to Congress as a Democrat in 1852, and he had voted against the Kansas-Nebraska Act. But he had won as a Know Nothing in 1854. Had all the northerners and southerners originally elected as Know Nothings cooperated when Congress met, they could probably have elected the Speaker of the House. But now northern Know Nothings, just like anti-Nebraska Whigs, insisted that the Speaker must be a northern opponent of the Kansas-Nebraska Act. Banks filled the bill, and most northerners rallied behind him on ballot after ballot during December and January until he was finally elected by a plurality vote in late January. Jubilant Republicans called his election "a great triumph for the North" and a "demonstration of the fact that we håd a party." Coupled with a successful national Republican organizational meeting in Pittsburgh on February 22, Banks's victory signaled that the exclusively northern and overtly anti-southern Republican Party was a rising force with which to be reckoned. It was also, of course, precisely the kind of sectional party that Franklin Pierce had long condemned as a threat to the Union he loved.

In the lengthy annual message Pierce sent to Congress at the end of December 1855, he remained totally mum about the political catastrophe that had befallen the Democratic Party in the past two years' elections. Much of that message, as noted in the preceding chapter, dealt with the ongoing dispute with Great Britain over Central America and the recent attempt by British officials in the United States to recruit Americans for British military forces in the Crimean War. But Pierce also attacked the anti-Nebraska and antisouthern message of the anti-Democratic political forces that had surged in the North since the introduction of the Kansas-Nebraska Act. The Missouri Compromise's prohibition of slavery north of the thirty-six-thirty line, he insisted, was of "doubtful constitutionality." It "had been practically abrogated by the legislation attending the organization of Utah, New Mexico, and Washington." Thus, the effective repeal of that prohibition in the Kansas-Nebraska Act was both "manly and ingenuous." Its repeal "was the final consummation and complete recognition of that principle that no portion of the United States [i.e., the North] shall undertake through assumption of the powers of the General Government to dictate the social institutions of any other portion." Northern cries that the law constituted a "breach of faith" were "utterly destitute of substantial justification." Nor did cries of Slave Power aggressions against the North hold water. "At the present time, this reputed aggression, resting, as it does, in the vague declamatory charges of political agitators," was both false and dangerous to the perpetuity of the Union.

Pierce openly sided with the South. He also declared war on the organizing principles of the new Republican Party. The question, as he entered the last year of his four-year term, was whether his actions and those of his fellow Democratic Party members in 1856 would continue to fan or undercut the growth of this new northern party.

5

Defeat

On November 1, 1855, two months before Pierce sent his third annual message to the Senate, he asked his assembled cabinet members whether he should seek renomination at the Democrats' 1856 national convention. They unanimously urged him to do so. Historians do not know whether he ever discussed this decision with Jane, but it seems unlikely given her continuing detestation of politics and life in Washington. Pierce's decision to seek another term was driven, in part, by a desire for vindication against the escalating criticism of his administration from opponents both inside and outside the Democratic Party. He also seemed to believe that he was the Democrat most capable of resolving the nation's domestic and foreign problems and thus to save his cherished Union.

Nonetheless, Pierce's decision raises two significant questions. Why, given the widespread anger among Democrats at his administration's patronage allocation, to say nothing of the thrashing Democratic candidates had suffered at the polls in 1854 and early 1855, did Pierce think he had a realistic chance of achieving renomination? By November 1855 he well knew that some Democrats had already been talking up Stephen A.

Douglas or James Buchanan as more "available"—that is, more likely to win—Democratic candidates. Why, moreover, unless he was totally delusional, did he think he had a chance of winning reelection even if he won renomination?

One answer to the first question is that certain elements in the Democratic Party wanted him to run again. None were more enthusiastic than Democratic newspaper editors in the South, especially the Deep South. They had been praising Pierce to the skies for more than two years, and well into the spring of 1856 they urged his renomination. Northern Free Soilers attacked Pierce, argued the Democratic sheet in Jackson, Mississippi, in February 1854, because "he interprets rightly the philosophy of the Baltimore platform, and has manifested an unyielding determination to stand upon that covenant, though he himself should fall in attempting to maintain it in its integrity. He is a lion in the pathway of the fanatics." "No Chief Magistrate has ever so fully thrown the weight of his official position, and brought to bear so unreservedly the influence of administration in favor of the South against the fanatics and fanaticism of the North," echoed a Mobile, Alabama, Democratic editor in November 1855. "Mr. Pierce takes as his guide the Constitution, limited by the doctrine of strict construction, confining the Federal Government to the exercise of none but clearly delegated powers, which is fatal to Abolitionism and all other isms that threaten the Union and our rights in the Union."

Some New England Democrats also endorsed his renomination. Later that November, Pierce's secretary, Sidney Webster, successfully enlisted the chairman of the New Hampshire state Democratic committee to secure a resolution demanding Pierce's nomination from the party's state convention, which met in December. Democrats from Massachusetts, Rhode Island, and Vermont also backed his renomination. Together, delegations from the Deep South and New England provided a base on which Pierce could presumably build a convention victory.

Pierce's belief that he could win reelection if he won renomination, in turn, reflected a misreading of the political situation. After Democratic defeats in the three New England states in the spring of 1855, Democratic candidates enjoyed a minor comeback. Most of the subsequent contests during the remainder of the year occurred in the South, where Democrats rebuffed the Know Nothing challenge in all but three states. Yet Democrats also achieved some success in elections for minor state offices in New Jersey and Pennsylvania and even in Maine's gubernatorial election. What success Democrats achieved in the North, however, could primarily be attributed to the failure of their polyglot opponents to combine behind a single ticket. In early November 1855 Pierce did not foresee that the various anti-Nebraska men in the new Congress would ultimately unite behind and elect Nathaniel P. Banks as Speaker of the House, thus signifying the coalescence of the Democratic Party's northern opponents behind a potentially powerful Republican Party.

The growth of the Republican Party during the first half of 1856, based primarily on hostility to the Kansas-Nebraska Act, was the shoal on which Pierce's hopes for renomination foundered. The longer the impending presidential campaign appeared likely to focus on Kansas, the larger the number of northern Democrats grew who believed it would be suicidal to run Pierce in 1856; he was too prominently associated with the act. Conversely, because James Buchanan had been in England during 1854 and 1855, he escaped any personal responsibility for the administration's policy toward Kansas, and the more he appeared to be the safest candidate to growing numbers of northern—as well as southern—Democrats.

During the fall of 1855, after the adjournment of the pro-slavery territorial legislature, Kansas had assumed a misleading appearance of tranquillity. From the start of 1856 until the meeting of the Democratic national convention on June 2, however, events in or about Kansas doomed Pierce's bid. On January 15, even before Banks's election as Speaker, dissident northerners in Kansas held elections to establish the "free state" government to rival the official territorial government elected in March 1855. This defiant action forced Pierce to take a public stand, one that seemed overtly prosouthern. In a message to Congress dated January 24, 1856, Pierce blamed the confusion in Kansas primarily on his first choice for territorial governor, Andrew H. Reeder, who had delayed the elections for the territorial legislature, and then its first meeting, in order to pursue his speculations. He admitted that Missourians had interfered in the legislative elections but justified their interference as a reaction to attempts by abolitionist groups in the Northeast to "colonize" the territory. In any event, he contended, "Whatever irregularities may have occurred in the elections, it seems too late now to raise that question. . . . For all present purposes the legislative body thus constituted and elected was the legitimate legislative assembly of the Territory." Hence the attempt to establish a "free state" government in defiance of that legislature was not just "illegal"; it was "revolutionary." "It will become treasonable insurrection if it reach the length of organized resistance by force to the fundamental or any other Federal law and to the authority of the General Government." Consequently, "it will be my imperative duty to exert the whole power of the Federal Executive to support public order in the Territory; to vindicate its laws, whether Federal or local, against all attempts at organized resistance, and so protect its people in the establishment of their own institutions."

Pierce followed this message with a proclamation, issued on February 11, that ordered the members of the new "free state" government "to disperse and retire peaceably to their respective abodes." It also warned that "any attempted insurrection" against the territorial government "would be resisted not only by the employment of the local militia, but also by that of any available forces of the United States." Pierce was throwing the weight of the federal government, including its military forces, behind the illegally elected proslavery territorial legislature, which had brazenly deprived northern settlers in Kansas of fundamental civil rights and was determined to make Kansas a new slave state. If anything more were necessary to destroy Pierce's electability in most of the North, this was it.

The next shoe fell on February 22, when two different political meetings were held at the opposite ends of Pennsylvania. In Pittsburgh the still embryonic Republican Party, which did not yet exist in several northern states, made its first attempt at forming a national organization. Every free state, as well as Kansas and Nebraska territories, sent representatives. They adopted a platform that among other things pledged to oust the Pierce administration from power and instructed a newly appointed national committee to draft a call for delegates to attend a presidential nominating convention in Philadelphia on June 17. That call invited all Americans "who are opposed to the repeal of the Missouri Compromise, to the policy of the present Administration, [and] to the extension of Slavery into the Territories" to elect delegates to that convention. Republicans explicitly presented themselves as the anti-Pierce party.

Meanwhile, the Know Nothings' national nominating convention in Philadelphia fractured along sectional lines over the slavery extension issue. Most northern delegates stomped out in disgust when the convention nominated former president

Millard Fillmore and when its national platform failed to call for repeal of the Kansas-Nebraska Act and for reimposition of the 1820 ban on slavery north of the thirty-six-thirty line. Dubbing themselves North Americans, they called for a separate party nominating convention in New York City, one week before the Republican national convention was scheduled to meet. The bolt of northern Know Nothings did not assure Republicans that they might join forces with their new party, which styled itself the defender of northerners' rights against Slave Power aggressions. It did, however, enhance the chances that North Americans might do so.

In May, scarcely two weeks before Democrats convened in Cincinnati, that assurance ultimately came. Friction between the official territorial and "free state" governments in Kansas, both of which were heavily armed, was almost inevitable. One flashpoint concerned men accused of violating the laws of one government who paid fealty to the other, whether or not those violations had anything to do with slavery. This was the case when the proslavery legislature sent a posse, including many Missourians, to arrest several "free state" leaders in the town of Lawrence, Kansas, on May 21, 1856. The posse terrorized the townsfolk, destroyed the printing press of an antislavery newspaper, and shelled a stoutly built hotel with cannon fire. No blood was shed, yet this "invasion," immediately labeled the "Sack of Lawrence," provided grist for the Republican propaganda mill in northeastern states. "The War Actually Begun—Triumph of the Border Ruffians—Lawrence in Ruins—Several Persons Slaughtered—Freedom Bloodily Subdued," hyperbolized the eastern Republican press.

Two days before this incident, on May 19, 1856, Charles Sumner, a Massachusetts Republican senator with Free Soil antecedents, began a carefully rehearsed and extraordinarily vituperative two-day speech on the Senate floor called "The

Crime against Kansas." In it he attacked the South, the state of South Carolina, and, in wantonly cruel language, South Carolina's senior senator Andrew Pickens Butler, who had temporarily returned to his home state. Southerners in Washington were furious, and one of them, Representative Preston S. Brooks of South Carolina, a distant cousin of Butler, determined to avenge the insult to his state and his family. On May 22, he entered the Senate chamber, accosted Sumner who sat at his desk, and beat him into bloody unconsciousness with a gutta-percha cane. No other incident in 1856 so enraged the North or ensured that most northern Know Nothings would indeed enlist in the Republicans' antisouthern crusade. The more potent the Republican Party appeared in the North, the more remote were Pierce's chances of obtaining the Democrats' presidential nomination.

Yet it was not just events related to Kansas that undermined Pierce's chances. Rancorous intraparty factionalism also hurt. Both of Virginia's U.S. senators supported Pierce, but the chairman of Virginia's delegation to the Cincinnati convention, Governor Henry Wise, supported Buchanan. And Wise had gained so much credit from Virginia Democrats for reversing the Know Nothing tide in the state's 1855 gubernatorial election that his opposition to Pierce could prove decisive, no matter what the two senators wanted.

New York was another state whose convention vote seemed in play. Pierce had sided with New York's Soft-Shells in squabbles over patronage in the Empire State, and they strongly supported his renomination. That support, if nothing else, drove Daniel Dickinson, the Hards' leader, to back Buchanan, the man whose nomination Pierce most wanted to block. The two factions held separate state conventions in 1856 and sent separate delegations to Cincinnati. From Pierce's perspective, therefore, much depended on which delegation the convention seated. Its decision to seat both and give each delegate a one-half vote effectively deprived him of New York's support.

Finally, credible reports that Pierce's managers had entered into negotiations with those of Stephen A. Douglas prior to the convention to cooperate against Buchanan caused Indiana's Democratic senator Jesse D. Bright, one of the most unsavory characters ever to serve in the Senate, and who was jealous of Douglas, to support Buchanan in Cincinnati and to turn the Indiana delegation, as well as those of a few other midwestern states, against Douglas and Pierce.

The combination of these developments caused James Gordon Bennett, the editor of the *New York Herald* who had been savaging Pierce since 1853, to pronounce an epitaph on Pierce's chances on May 29, 1856, five days before the national convention opened. "Pierce's follies, his imbecilities, his false promises, and still falser associates, have ruined him with his own party. He is now merely a dupe in their hands." A few days later, the hostile Republican *New York Times* echoed that judgment in an editorial. Although it, like its reporters in Cincinnati, expected Buchanan to win the nomination in a cakewalk, it opined that "the only certainty appears to be that PIERCE will be thrown overboard at once, as a political Jonah, and the South is not so fishy as to make an attempt to swallow him."

Perhaps a better index of Pierce's current standing in the North, however, occurred in his hometown of Concord, New Hampshire. In late May its residents, who had purchased a magnificent horse for Pierce when he went off to Mexico in 1847, now burned him in effigy along with Preston Brooks.

. . .

The newspaper predictions about an immediate abandonment of Pierce at the Cincinnati convention proved erroneous. The convention opened on June 2 but did not begin balloting for the presidential nominee until June 5. In the meantime the credentials committee had to resolve disputes between contesting delegations from Missouri and New York, and the latter was not resolved until the morning of June 5 itself. The convention also adopted the party's national platform before the nomination balloting began. Its most important plank endorsed the Kansas-Nebraska Act on precisely the same grounds as Pierce had taken—namely, that it embodied the principle of congressional noninterference that was articulated by the Compromise of 1850 and endorsed by the nation in 1852. Other planks denounced the bigotry of the Know Nothings, condemned the antisouthern sectional agitation of the Republicans for endangering the Union, and charged the next administration with ensuring "the ascendancy" of the United States in the Gulf of Mexico. Intriguingly, the resolutions committee that wrote the platform initially defeated a resolution offered by the member from Maryland praising the Pierce administration, only to adopt a similar one with the crucial caveat that it not be presented to the convention until after the balloting for the presidential nominee was over—that is, when it would do Pierce no good.

Nomination by the Democratic national convention required a two-thirds majority. On the first ballot, Buchanan failed to get even a simple majority. He led the count with 135 votes, but Pierce ran a respectable second with 122 while Douglas obtained 33 and Lewis Cass a mere 5. Pierce won 26 of New England's 41 votes, with Buchanan capturing the others, including a majority of Maine's and all of Connecticut's. Virginia, Louisiana, Delaware, and three-fourths of Maryland's votes went to Buchanan, as did a minority of Kentucky's. Nonetheless, Pierce outpolled Buchanan 74 to 34 among slave-state delegations, while Missouri cast its 9 votes for Douglas. North Carolina, South Carolina, Georgia, Alabama, Tennessee, Arkansas, Florida, and Texas voted for Pierce unanimously. New York split down the middle, casting 17 votes for Buchanan and 18 for Pierce. Over half of Buchanan's total came from just three states: Pennsylvania, Ohio, and Indiana.

Pierce's initial support did not instantly melt away as pundits had predicted. Over the next four ballots his support held steady at 119 votes while Buchanan's inched above 140, still shy of a simple majority let alone the necessary two-thirds. On the sixth ballot Tennessee shifted its 12 votes from Pierce to Buchanan, although on the very next ballot it switched them to Douglas. Tennessee's defection from the Pierce column led to a perceptible decline in his support. By the seventh ballot he was down to 89, and by the fifteenth and last ballot held on June 5, he fell to 79 as Buchanan and Douglas climbed to 152 and 63 votes, respectively. Telegraphic dispatches had kept Pierce abreast of the events in Cincinnati, and that night he wired his New Hampshire floor managers to withdraw his name the following morning. His bid for renomination was over.

Pierce hoped and expected that most of his supporters would shift to Douglas in order to stop Buchanan, and on the first ballot on June 6 Douglas's support rose to 121 votes. Still, Buchanan led with 168. From Washington, Douglas telegraphed William A. Richardson, the chairman of the Illinois delegation, to withdraw his name, in part because he had received assurances from Buchanan's managers that they would support his nomination in 1860. That withdrawal ended the contest; on the seventeenth and final ballot Buchanan was unanimously nominated as the Democrats' contender for the presidency. Only after that result did the convention adopt the platform plank that praised Pierce and his administration, although one Indiana delegate protested that "he would never consent that the great North-West should be slandered and stultified by the supposition that she endorsed the Administration of Franklin Pierce."

The convention still had to nominate a vice presidential candidate, and on the first ballot ten men received votes. John A. Quitman of Mississippi led with 59 votes; John C. Breckinridge of Kentucky, who was at the convention, followed closely with 55. That both men were well-known friends of Pierce was probably no coincidence. The nomination was a bone tossed by the victorious Buchanan men to the defeated Pierce forces, and on the second ballot, after the Mississippi delegation had withdrawn Quitman's name, Breckinridge received the nomination.

"Poor Pierce," mocked the hostile *New York Times* in an editorial several days after the convention closed. "With all the resources of the Government at his command, [he] has been unable to secure for himself the empty honor of renomination. He was taken up, in the first place, because he was unknown, and now he is spurned because he is known." "What a book he might write about the ingratitude of parties!" The historian can only imagine the depths of Pierce's personal disappointment, but publicly he reacted to the outcome at Cincinnati with characteristic graciousness. When a crowd of celebrating Democrats that included both Stephen Douglas and Lewis Cass came by a few days after the convention closed, he gave them an impromptu address from a White House window. He urged Democrats to pull together behind the ticket in order to save the Union. He would happily return to private life in New Hampshire, he avowed, "with a consciousness of having adopted no single measure of public policy during my administration which I did not believe to be demanded by the best interests of the country, nor one which does not, tonight, command the approbation of my judgment and my conscience." Pierce closed his speech by predicting a Democratic victory in the fall if all

Democrats rallied behind the principles enunciated in the party's platform, which, he stressed, were the same principles to which he had adhered during his administration.

. . .

Four days after the close of the Cincinnati convention, and with the meeting of the North American convention in New York City, a series of political maneuvers began that would challenge Pierce's confident prediction of Democratic victory. The Sack of Lawrence and the brutal caning of Senator Sumner enhanced the chances of a merger between northern Know Nothings and Republicans, but such a coalition required the mutually suspicious leadership of the two organizations to agree upon a common presidential candidate. Shrewd Republican politicos such as New York's Thurlow Weed were especially concerned that the North Americans would jump first to nominate a candidate whom the Republicans would then be forced to embrace, thus alienating hundreds of thousands of northern voters who considered most Know Nothings bigoted thugs. So the wily Weed devised a brilliant stratagem. He persuaded the North Americans to nominate Speaker of the House Nathaniel P. Banks for president.

But what neither he nor Banks himself told the delegates was that Banks was to be a stalking horse for a different Republican nominee whom the Know Nothings would then be forced to endorse in order to bring about the merger. The plan worked like a charm. The North Americans nominated Banks, who made no response to the convention until after the Republicans nominated John C. Frémont at Philadelphia. Then Banks declined the North Americans' nomination and urged them to back Frémont, which they grudgingly did, although a dispute about which party's vice presidential nominee should be on the ticket with Frémont was not settled until late August. The most conservative northern Know Nothings continued to support Millard Fillmore, who received a separate nomination from a rump Whig convention in September, but the vast majority of the Democratic Party's northern opponents had been united behind the Republican banner. November's results would show what a potent political combine had been created.

As a sitting president and now a lame duck for the remaining nine months of his term, Pierce played no direct role in the ensuing campaign. But his actions as president surely affected it. In May he had vetoed three internal improvement bills, and in August he nixed two additional bills. With Pierce now largely impotent, Congress overrode the vetoes. Kansas, however, remained the administration's and the Democratic Party's biggest headache.

No blood had been shed during the Sack of Lawrence, but a few nights later, apparently in retaliation for this raid, the antislavery fanatic John Brown and his sons butchered five innocent settlers along Pottawatomie Creek in Franklin County, Kansas. Not one of the victims owned slaves; their offense was that they paid fealty to the official territorial legislature. During the summer, armed skirmishes between those loyal to the territorial legislature and those aligned with the "free state" government erupted, although there was far more marching and countermarching than serious fighting. In any event, Governor Wilson Shannon proved increasingly ineffective in keeping the peace. In contrast, Colonel Edwin Sumner, commander of the regular army troops in Kansas, proved, if anything, too effective in dealing with the "free state" government that Pierce had declared insurrectionary. He arrested its elected governor, Charles Robinson, on a charge of treason and dispersed the first meeting of the "free state" legislature on July 4, 1856—actions that allowed Republicans to charge that the army sided with proslavery men.

The longer "Bleeding Kansas" remained in the public eye, the more the Republicans benefited. In his message to Congress in January 1856, Pierce had said that the best solution for the troubles in Kansas was to admit it to statehood as soon as it had the requisite population. On offense Republicans vainly cried for its immediate admission as a free state. In June Georgia's onetime Whig but now Democratic senator Robert Toombs introduced a bill that went Pierce one better. It called for waiving the population requirement, moving for immediate Kansas statehood, and holding an election in Kansas for delegates to a state constitutional convention. The election would be monitored by a federal commission that would ensure that this time only legitimate residents of Kansas voted. The Senate passed this sensible measure by a vote of thirty-one to thirteen, but the Republican majority in the House refused to consider it. "All these gentlemen want is to get up murder and bloodshed in Kansas for political effect," Stephen Douglas accurately protested in a Senate speech. "They do not mean that there shall be peace until after the presidential election. . . . An angel from heaven could not write a bill to restore peace in Kansas that would be acceptable to the Abolition Republican party previous to the presidential election."

Absent action by Congress that might resolve the turbulent situation in Kansas, the responsibility fell to Pierce and his administration. He sent another army officer to replace Sumner as commander of federal troops in the territory, and in late July he appointed John W. Geary of Pennsylvania to replace the feckless Shannon as territorial governor. This appointment was a ten-strike. A veteran of the Mexican-American War who had seen much combat, the imposingly tall and decisive Geary, with the help of the new army commander Persifor Smith, managed to restore order to Kansas when he reached the territory in the fall. By then, however, the political damage to the

Democratic Party had already been done. "Bleeding Kansas" and "Bleeding Sumner" had given Republicans almost invincible electoral slogans.

Almost is the key word here, for in November James Buchanan won the three-way race for president. He won with only 45 percent of the popular vote and largely because he carried every slave state but Maryland, Millard Fillmore's lone trophy. It was the North, however, that best reflected the political reaction to Franklin Pierce's presidency. In 1852 Pierce had carried fourteen of the sixteen free states. In 1856 Buchanan won but five—California, Illinois, Indiana, Pennsylvania, and New Jersey—while Republicans carried the remaining eleven. Of the northern states Buchanan won, moreover, he eked out a bare majority of the popular vote in only two: Indiana and Pennsylvania. Had all the opponents of Pierce's administration aligned behind a single candidate rather than dividing between Frémont and Fillmore, the Democrats would have lost the other three as well.

The voter realignment against the Democratic Party was especially marked in the upper North. Pierce had swept his home state of New Hampshire in 1852 with almost 57 percent of the popular vote; in 1856 Frémont carried it with 53.7 percent while Buchanan garnered less than 46 percent. Or take Michigan and Wisconsin, the states where the Republican Party had first formed in 1854. Pierce had carried the former with 50.4 percent of the vote and the latter with 52 percent in the three-way contest of 1852. Buchanan won only 41.5 percent of Michigan's vote and 44.2 percent in Wisconsin.

The region-wide figures are more stunning. In 1852 Pierce had won 49.8 percent of the North's popular vote. In 1856 Buchanan earned only 41.4 percent. It is true that the Democrats ran considerably better in the North's congressional elections in 1856 than they had in 1854. To give but one example,

Democrats won eight House seats in Ohio in 1856—largely because Know Nothings and Republicans split the anti-Democratic vote—whereas their total in 1854 was zero. Regardless, this indicated a massive swing of the northern electorate against the Democratic Party and a telling index of what Franklin Pierce had done to it.

One other aspect of the 1856 presidential election merits emphasis. Millard Fillmore won almost four hundred thousand votes in the North, and in three states his support helped Buchanan to victory. Yet that total was less than a third of the vote amassed by Frémont in the free states. In the words of William E. Gienapp, the foremost historian of the Republican Party's origins, 1856 constituted a "victorious defeat" for the Republicans, for the results clearly indicated that the Republicans, and not the Know Nothings, had displaced the Whigs as Democrats' major party foe, that Republicans were the party of the future for anyone who wanted to punish Democrats at the polls. By 1860 almost all of Fillmore's northern supporters had moved into the Republican column, and their conversion helps explain why Abraham Lincoln won.

· · ·

There is no evidence that Pierce ever conceded that he personally was largely responsible for the damage done to the northern wing of the Democratic Party. In the final annual message he sent to Congress on December 2, 1856, he attributed the nation's and his party's troubles to an old enemy: antislavery fanatics in the North who endangered the Union. This message—surely one of the most bitter and intemperate ever sent to Congress—deserves extensive quotation.

Pierce began by seeming to deny that the Democratic Party was imperiled in the North. In the recent election, he averred, Americans had asserted "the constitutional equality of each and all of the States of the Union as States." They had "maintained the inviolability of the constitutional rights of the different sections of the Union" and reaffirmed their commitment to the Constitution and the Union. "In doing this," he continued, "they have at the same time emphatically condemned the idea of organizing in these United States mere geographical parties, of marshalling in hostile array toward each other the different parts of the country, North or South, East or West."

Yet Pierce recognized that the overtly antisouthern Republican Party was no mere phantasm. Political "associations" had been formed in some northern states by "individuals who, pretending to seek only to prevent the spread of the institution of slavery into the present or future inchoate States of the Union, are really inflamed with desire to change the domestic institutions of existing States." They dedicated "themselves to the odious task of depreciating the government organization which stands in their way and of calumniating with indiscriminate invective not only the citizens of particular States with whose laws they find fault, but all others of their fellow citizens throughout the country who do not participate with them in their assaults upon the Constitution." Their objective of abolition was "revolutionary," and it would lead "inevitably into mutual devastation and fratricidal carnage." Still, "they endeavor to prepare the people of the United States for civil war by doing everything in their power to deprive the Constitution and the laws of their moral authority and to undermine the fabric of the Union by appeals to passion and sectional prejudice, by indoctrinating its people with reciprocal hatred." For years they had acted "aggressively against the constitutional rights of nearly one-half of the thirty-one States."

To prove this charge, Pierce treated Congress to his version of American history. He began with the formation of abolitionist societies that he had first denounced in the 1830s. Next on his list was northern resistance to the Fugitive Slave Act of 1850. Then came a truly "revisionist" explanation of the repeal of the 1820 prohibition against slavery extension north of the thirty-six-thirty line in the Louisiana Territory. That ban, he falsely alleged, "was acquiesced in rather than approved by the States of the Union." When northerners in the 1840s had refused to extend the line to the new Mexican Cession, they had "repeal[ed] it as a legislative compromise," and thereafter "this enactment ceased to have binding virtue in any sense" as the territorial provisions of the Compromise of 1850 proved.

The sophistry of this analysis is breathtaking. In 1820, as compensation for allowing Missouri's admission as a slave state, every southerner in the Senate and a majority of them in the House had agreed to divide the remainder of the Louisiana Purchase Territory at the thirty-six-thirty line, with slavery allowed south of it and forever prohibited north of it. This line applied exclusively to that geographic area, not any other. Pierce was arguing that northerners' refusal to extend the line to a different geographic area in the 1840s repealed the sectional agreement over the line within the Louisiana Territory. But his inventive history was just beginning.

By 1854, when the territories of Kansas and Nebraska were organized, it had "come to be seen clearly that Congress does not possess constitutional power to impose restrictions of this character upon any present or future State of the Union." Pierce never mentioned the Republican Party by name in this message, but in these words he dismissed the party's central policy objective—congressional prohibition of slavery from territories—as unconstitutional. In any event, Pierce continued, complaints that repeal of the 1820 prohibition violated a sacred compact were bogus. Congress had the right to repeal any law it had previously enacted. "The repeal in terms of a statute, which was already obsolete and also null for unconstitutionality, could have no influence to obstruct or to promote the propagation of conflicting views of political or social institutions." In fact, "all the repeal did was to relieve the statute book of an objectionable enactment, unconstitutional in effect and injurious in terms to a large portion of the States." Little wonder that southern Democrats loved Pierce!

Finally, Pierce turned to the situation in Kansas. Here his prosouthern tilt was even more marked. "Revolutionary disorder in Kansas had its origin in [northern] projects of intervention . . . and when propagandist colonization of Kansas had thus been undertaken in one section of the Union for the systematic promotion of its peculiar view of policy there ensued as a matter of course a counteraction with opposite views in other sections of the Union." It was true that Missourians bent on supporting the proslavery territorial legislature had repeatedly intervened in Kansas, Pierce admitted, but northern outsiders who supported its opponents in Kansas had also poured in from Iowa. More important—and here Pierce was absolutely correct—"the difficulties in that Territory have been extravagantly exaggerated for purposes of political agitation elsewhere." "Irregularities" in Kansas elections "were beyond the sphere of action of the Executive." In contrast, he boasted, "the attempt of a part of the inhabitants of the Territory to erect a revolutionary government, though sedulously encouraged and supplied with pecuniary aid from active agents of disorder in some of the States [i.e., the North], has failed." And the military had expelled armed outsiders. Pierce rejoiced in "the peaceful condition of things in Kansas, especially considering the means to which it was necessary to have recourse for the attainment of the end."

But his defense of his actions did not end there. Sectional conflict over slavery in Kansas was "inevitable." "No human prudence, no form of legislation, no wisdom on the part of

Congress, could have prevented it. It is idle to suppose that the particular provisions of the organic law were the cause of the agitation." That agitation "was inherent in the nature of things." What was more, he ended, northerners who faulted him for failing to stop Border Ruffians' illegal interventions into elections within Kansas were mistaken. It was up to the people themselves to guarantee that elections were honest and fair. Local elections were beyond the purview of a president's constitutional authority.

Thus in his valedictory address to Congress and the nation, Franklin Pierce exempted himself from any personal responsibility for the reverses suffered by the northern Democratic Party and the escalating sectional conflict over slavery extension that afflicted his beloved Union. That conflict, after all, "was inherent in the nature of things." What this historian, at least, does not know is whether Pierce actually believed what he had written.

6

Retirement

Franklin Pierce was fifty-two years old when he left the White House in March 1857. He would live another twelve years. During his four years as president he had earned an annual salary of $25,000, comparable to $500,000 per year in current dollars, and in an era without income taxes he had managed to save more than half of what he had earned. These savings had been shrewdly invested in railroad and bank stocks and bonds as well as profitable land speculation by his Concord law partner Josiah Minot. As a result, Pierce was worth $78,000, or more than $1.5 million in current dollars, when he left the presidency. He had no need or desire to resume the practice of law. Instead, he intended to take care of the chronically ill Jane. Some years later, indeed, when a close friend, Clarence March, asked him why he had ever married such an invalid, Pierce forthrightly replied, "I could take better care of her than anyone else."

Jane was so enfeebled by a recurrent bout with tuberculosis in March 1857 that the Pierces remained in the capital for three weeks after Buchanan's inauguration. They stayed with William L. Marcy in the house he had rented. Both Pierce and

Marcy despised Buchanan, and they were especially incensed that Buchanan made it clear early on that he intended to replace every Democratic federal officeholder appointed by Pierce with other Democrats loyal to himself. Nor did Buchanan ever speak a word to Vice President Breckinridge, a Pierce man, for the first three years of his administration. Pierce never uttered a public criticism of Buchanan; Marcy was not so reticent. He was quoted in a March issue of the *New York Herald* as complaining, "Well, they have it that I am the author of the office seekers' doctrine, that 'to the victors belong the spoils'; but I certainly should never recommend the policy of pillaging my own camp."

Pierce's stay at Marcy's house allowed scores of Democrats to pay their respects to this congenial party leader of whom they were genuinely fond. "I venture to say," Marcy later wrote, "no occupants of the White House ever left Washington with such deep feelings of affection from the people of this city." No president, he added, had ever excelled Pierce in "the art of winning hearts." On March 25, the Pierces finally took a train from Washington to Philadelphia, where they stayed for six weeks in a hotel while Jane consulted with a doctor. The physician had been recommended by James Campbell, whose wife was dying of tuberculosis. During this time, Jane appeared to recover enough to take several horseback rides, and on May 20 they took the train to New York City, where they spent a week in the home of former Whig governor and senator Hamilton Fish.

Pierce finally reached New Hampshire in early June after dropping Jane off at her sister's home in Andover, Massachusetts, the place where Jane had taken refuge after Benny's death. Pierce moved into the old family estate in Hillsborough rather than renting the house in Concord, and later that summer Jane joined him at a hotel in Portsmouth so they could be close to the sea. The months there were punctuated by the deaths of colleagues and friends. Marcy, whom Pierce considered "a firm and confiding friend," died on July 4, and Pierce, along with former president Martin Van Buren, attended the funeral in Albany. Then in August came word that James C. Dobbin and Abby Means, Jane's cousin and close friend who had served as White House hostess during the first two years of Pierce's administration, had died on the same day.

The most consequential development during Pierce's stay in Portsmouth, however, was that he met and instantly befriended Clarence March, who was eleven years younger than Pierce and the brother of Charles March, who had once read law in Pierce's Concord office. (March would remain close to Pierce until his death in 1869, and a diary he kept is one of the best sources of information about Pierce during his retirement.) When out of Jane's sight, the two new friends engaged in some epic drinking bouts, alternately consuming large quantities of brandy and champagne. March helped to arrange a warm place for the Pierces to live so that Jane could escape the harsh New England winter. His uncle was the American consul to Madeira, and March persuaded his uncle to take in the couple.

The Pierces secured free passage on a U.S. Navy vessel and arrived in Madeira in late December 1857. They stayed in John Howard March's apparently spacious house on the island for the next six months. Jane's health improved markedly, and within weeks she was taking rides on one of the two horses Pierce had brought with them while Pierce went off alone on even longer rides across the island. Aside from rest and rehabilitation, their other big project during this prolonged sojourn was an attempt to learn French in preparation for a planned tour of the Continent. Frank picked up the language more easily than Jane.

Starting in June 1858 they visited Portugal, Spain, France, and Switzerland. Late that fall they moved to Florence, Naples, and Capri, Italy, and finally in February 1859 they traveled to Rome for a long anticipated reunion with Nathaniel Hawthorne. Pierce had appointed Hawthorne as American consul to Liverpool, and he had remained at his post until he was replaced by a Buchanan favorite. Hawthorne moved to Rome in the fall of 1858, and Pierce had not seen his friend in nearly six years.

The Pierces found Hawthorne and his wife, Sophia, almost paralyzed with anxiety about the failing health of their teenage daughter, Una. To take Hawthorne's mind off his troubles, Pierce insisted that the novelist accompany him on walks around Rome. After Una recovered, Sophia wrote that Pierce had "wrapped [Hawthorne] around with the most soothing care." Hawthorne himself later recalled, "Never having had any trouble before, that pierced into my very vitals, I did not know what comfort there might be in the manly sympathy of a friend, but Pierce has undergone so great a sorrow of his own, and has so large and kindly a heart, and is so tender and strong that he really did us good, and I shall always love him better for the recollection of those dark days."

The good turn in Una Hawthorne's health allowed the Pierces to resume the remainder of their planned tour of Europe even though Jane's health began to fail once again. From Rome they went to Venice, then to Vienna and to Germany where Jane saw doctors, then to Paris via Brussels, and finally to London. They sailed for the United States in mid-August and arrived at Norfolk, Virginia, in September. By September 11, 1859, they had reached Jane's family in Andover, with whom Jane once again made a long stay.

• • •

By then it was apparent that Buchanan's administration was a disaster. It reeked with corruption, and Republicans were readying themselves to air it in public. Buchanan had botched his heavy-handed attempt to force the admission of Kansas as a slave state. And he had mishandled the brief recession following the Panic of 1857, providing a potent goad to the opposition's demands for a higher protective tariff. Former members of Pierce's cabinet, including Jefferson Davis and Robert McClelland, and other Democrats urged him to seek the party's presidential nomination in 1860. Pierce would have none of it. "It would annoy me if I believed my name would come before the Charleston Convention under any possible combination of circumstances," he wrote one supporter in late September. After dining with Pierce, Clarence March noted, "He persists that he has no desire, and would not consent, to be President again."

What Pierce did want to do that fall was buy land in New Hampshire that he could farm. Throughout his years in the state legislature and Congress, Pierce had taken great joy in devoting summer recesses to the physical labor of farmwork on the family estate in Hillsborough. But his older brother Henry had inherited that farm, and Pierce wanted land of his own. In the fall of 1859, while Jane remained in Andover, he purchased a sixty-acre tract near the town center of Concord. His plan, never realized, was to build a house on a portion of the land and farm the rest of it. He managed only to farm some of those acres.

Jane's frail health still required finding a warm refuge for the winter, and they decided upon Nassau in the Bahamas. Before sailing from New York in January 1860, Pierce sent a letter to Jefferson Davis urging him to seek the Democrats' presidential nomination. He predicted that southern secession would make a bloody civil war inevitable, but "if through the madness of northern abolitionism that dire calamity must come, the fighting will not be along Mason and Dixon's line merely." Instead, he believed, violence would also break out within the North itself between defenders of southerners' constitutional rights and abolitionist fanatics. When Union troops occupied Davis's Mississippi plantation in 1863, they found Pierce's letter, and the Republican press would use it to portray Pierce as a copperhead traitor to the Union.

The Pierces did not return from Nassau until the middle of May 1860, well after the breakup of the Democratic national convention in Charleston, South Carolina, at which northern Democrats failed to secure the two-thirds majority necessary to settle the nomination on Stephen A. Douglas. Most southern delegates loathed Douglas because of his prominent role in preventing the admission of Kansas as a slave state under the Lecompton Constitution in 1858 and his repeated insistence, known as the "Freeport Doctrine," that a territorial legislature could prevent the admission of slavery simply by refusing to pass positive laws protecting property rights in slaves in that territory. Southerners at the convention therefore insisted that the party's national platform demand federal slave codes in all territories, a position northern Democrats deemed politically suicidal. A bitter platform fight ensued, and when southern delegates lost, many of them, primarily those from Deep South states, bolted the convention. Douglas's northern supporters initially welcomed that walkout, for they believed it made it easier to secure the necessary two-thirds majority among the remaining delegates. But the chairman of the convention, none other than Pierce's close friend Caleb Cushing, ruled that nomination required two-thirds of the original number of delegates, not just of those who remained in the convention hall. Douglas's nomination was an arithmetic impossibility.

The Charleston convention had adjourned without making any presidential nomination, and a new, or at least reassembled, convention was scheduled to meet in Baltimore in June. Douglas's friends again had a majority at this new convention, and when they refused to seat the delegations that had walked out in Charleston and instead tried to seat men chosen by the pro-Douglas minority of southern Democrats in those states, virtually all southerners left the gathering. The northerners nominated Douglas; the southerners, still in Baltimore, nominated Pierce's friend Vice President John C. Breckinridge as their own candidate. Only then did Buchanan, who hated Douglas because Douglas had foiled his effort to bring Kansas into the Union as a slave state, deign to speak to Breckinridge. More important, Buchanan ordered federal patronage holders in the North to campaign for Breckinridge and against Douglas.

Pierce thus returned from Nassau between the collapse of the Charleston convention and the beginning of the Baltimore one. To prevent another breakup, some Democrats pressed Pierce to allow his name to be placed on the floor as a compromise. Again Pierce demurred, unsuccessfully urging that Cushing should seek the nomination.

Obsessed as ever about preserving the unity of the Democratic Party, Pierce was dismayed by the outcome in Baltimore. Privately, he preferred Breckinridge to Douglas, but once it became clear that the large majority of New Hampshire Democrats were in the Douglas camp, he pleaded with his closest allies to refrain from supporting a separate electoral ticket for the Kentuckian.

Pierce, like most Democrats, understood that the Democratic split made the election of Abraham Lincoln highly likely, if not inevitable. In October his former postmaster general James Campbell begged him to accept a last-minute Democratic nomination if Douglas and Breckinridge could be persuaded to drop out of the race. That scenario was unlikely, but Pierce used his reply to Campbell to repeat his refusal to run.

"I could not consent to be a candidate. It would be unwise for the party, *and absolutely out of the question for myself.*" Pierce's efforts to keep New Hampshire Democrats unified largely succeeded, although he failed to prevent Republicans from handily carrying New Hampshire in November, just as they did all of the states in the upper North.

. . .

Pierce understood southerners' temperament far better than Lincoln and most Republicans. He knew that their threat to secede should Lincoln win the election was deadly serious, not a mere bluff. Yet after Lincoln's victory, Pierce did what he could to prevent or at least slow secession. He urged a member of Buchanan's cabinet to avoid coercion of any seceding state at all costs. "The first blow in that direction will be a blow fatal to even hope." When, in late November, John A. Campbell, an associate justice of the Supreme Court whom Pierce had appointed, asked Pierce to visit his home state of Alabama to reassure its citizens, Pierce, who was sick, begged off. Instead, he sent a public letter that was widely disseminated in the southern press. Hundreds of thousands of northerners, he told the citizens of Alabama, were still ready to defend southerners' rights. Don't imperil the Union "by inconsiderate haste," he pleaded. Allow northerners' time "for the casting out of fanaticism, and the enthronement of reason." "If we cannot live together in peace," he added, "then in peace and on just terms, let us separate." For this reason, when Buchanan dispatched troops on an unarmed merchant vessel to reinforce Fort Sumter in early January 1861, Pierce condemned it as an "idle, foolish, ill-advised, criminal thing." As the historian William W. Freehling demonstrates in his recent, brilliant analysis of the secession crisis, on this score Pierce was absolutely right.

Because of his poor health, finally, Pierce was forced to decline an urgent invitation to attend the Peace Convention held at Washington's Willard Hotel. His presence there, however, could not have made a difference in the convention's ultimate futility.

The firing on Fort Sumter on April 12, 1861, precipitated the civil war Pierce had long feared. For Pierce this event created an existential dilemma. Although he blamed Republicans for causing that war, his love for the Union his father had helped establish was the overriding emotion. In late April he told a crowd in Concord that "the question has resolved itself into one of patriotism and stern duty." Then, however, he added an important caveat that was misunderstood at the time. He would support a war to protect Washington and the North from a southern invasion. But, as he later wrote Thomas Seymour, his old Mexican-American War comrade, he could not support an aggressive northern war that intended to subjugate the South. In a letter to Jane that spring, Pierce was more emphatic. "My purpose, dearest, is irrevocably taken. I will never justify, sustain or in any way or to any extent uphold this cruel, heartless, aimless, unnecessary war. Madness and imbecility are in the ascendant. I shall not succumb to them. Come what may, I have no opinion to retract—no line of action to change."

Because so many northern Democrats, including Caleb Cushing and Daniel S. Dickinson, fully endorsed the Lincoln administration's war effort, Pierce's silence was notable. When he traveled to Michigan in the fall of 1861 to inspect some property he owned, a newspaper editor hoping to spoof Republican claims about the existence of pro-Confederate groups in the state fabricated a story that Pierce had come to Detroit to give aid and encouragement to these enemies of the government. Republicans sent this wholly bogus story to the State

Department, which at that time had charge of arresting apparently dangerous pro-Confederate sympathizers, and a clerk wrote Pierce to ask him about the story. Pierce exploded in rage. He could not believe that Secretary of State William H. Seward himself had not had the courtesy to write to a former president. Worse, the department apparently found these aspersions against his loyalty credible. Thus, on Christmas Eve, 1861, Pierce fired off an indignant letter to Seward. "It is not easy to conceive how any person could give credence to, or entertain for a moment, the idea that I am now, or have ever been connected with a 'secret league,' or *any* league, the object of which was, or is, the overthrow of the government of my country. . . . My loyalty will never be successfully impugned so long as I enjoy the constitutional rights which pertain to every citizen of the republic."

The Lincoln administration's seeming assault on those rights, with its suspension of habeas corpus and application of military law to the North—even though relatively few actual arrests of civilians occurred in that section—especially infuriated Pierce. He was equally dismayed by Lincoln's proclamations of emancipation, which, in Pierce's eyes, converted an unnecessary war to restore the Union into a totally unconstitutional abolitionist crusade. Yet until the spring of 1863 he never spoke or wrote a word of public criticism about Lincoln. Indeed, in early 1862 he sent Lincoln a very kind note of condolence and sympathy after Lincoln's son Willie died in the White House.

What pushed Pierce over the edge was the arrest and prosecution by military tribunal in the spring of 1863 of the Ohio Peace Democrat Clement L. Vallandigham for calling the war a failure—an arrest and prosecution that Lincoln defended. For Pierce, this violation of fundamental civil liberty was too much; hence he agreed to be the keynote speaker at a mass

Democratic rally in Concord, New Hampshire, on July 4, 1863. Addressing some twenty-five thousand people, Pierce issued a passionate defense of the right of free speech. "Who," he asked, "has clothed the President with power to dictate to any of us when we may or must speak, or be silent, and especially in relation to the conduct of any public servant? By what right does he presume to prescribe a formula of language for your lips or mine?" Then Pierce took a step too far. Like Vallandigham, he described the Union's war effort as "fearful, fruitless, [and] fateful." A reliance on armed force, he averred, could never produce peace. Talk about poor timing! Even as Pierce spoke, the telegraph was bringing word of the Union victory at Gettysburg, and in the following days it would report Ulysses S. Grant's capture of Vicksburg. Nonetheless, Pierce's speech was so popular among Democrats that some of his diehard friends urged him to seek the party's presidential nomination in 1864, forcing him once again to insist that he would never do it.

Months before the Democratic national convention in late August 1864, Pierce suffered two more grievous losses. During the first two years of the Civil War, he spent most of his days away from Jane. While she stayed at her sister's home in Andover, he traipsed around New England, alone or in the company of Clarence March. There can be no question that Pierce loved his wife. It is equally clear, however, that once they returned from Europe in September 1859 he seemed quite content to let Jane's sister deal with her moods and maladies. No hard evidence exists, but it is likely that his renewed thirst for alcohol helps explain their frequent separation. The couple did spend some weeks together on the Massachusetts seaside in the summer of 1863. In the fall, Jane returned to Andover, and she died there from tuberculosis on December 2, 1863, at the age of fifty-seven.

The ever-faithful Hawthorne attended the funeral in Andover and the subsequent burial in Concord. He described Pierce
as "overwhelmed with grief." The following spring, Hawthorne's own health began to fail rapidly. Sensing impending
death, he told his wife that he wanted to spend some of his
final days with his great friend Pierce, to whom he had dedicated his last book. Sophia Hawthorne agreed in the hope that
a trip with Pierce might revive Nathaniel's health. Alerting
Pierce that her husband was now so feeble that he needed help
getting off a train and into and out of carriages, she wrote, "I
would not trust him in any hands now except such gentle and
tender hands as yours." In May 1838, Benjamin French had
penned a similar testament to Pierce's extraordinary capacity
for empathy. At that time, Pierce had come to French's room to
discuss the death of a congressman the preceding day. "He
feels such things as sensibly as any man I ever saw," wrote
French, "& were I about to leave this world I would have Frank
Pierce at my pillow sooner than any other man I ever knew in
whose veins flowed none of my own blood. I never—no never,
shall forget his kind attentions to me when I was sick once in
this city."

Pierce met Hawthorne in Boston in early May and took him
to Concord to the house he rented. The plan was to take a carriage trip to Dixville Notch in far northern New Hampshire, a
town now famous on presidential election nights for submit-
ting the first returns in the nation. On the third day of that
trip, they stopped at a hotel in Plymouth, New Hampshire,
where they took adjoining rooms and kept the connecting door
open. Hawthorne died sometime that night between 10 P.M.
and 3 A.M.; Pierce discovered the corpse. That moment, to
quote what Hawthorne had earlier written about their time in
Rome, had to have "pierced [his] very vitals." Pierce sat with

Hawthorne's bereaved family at the funeral in Salem, Massachusetts. Later, when he reread all of Hawthorne's novels, he pronounced him the greatest writer America had yet produced.

The deaths of Jane and his friend Hawthorne engendered some of Franklin Pierce's most generous actions. He insisted on paying Hawthorne's son Julian's tuition for four years at Harvard College. He would also pay full college tuition for his brother Henry's two sons, although only one of them, a student at Princeton, managed to graduate. Yet, it also appears, these two deaths turned Pierce ever more avidly toward the solace of strong drink.

Pierce was living in the same Concord house that he and Jane had rented before his presidency when the war ended and Lincoln was assassinated. That latter event brought an angry crowd to Pierce's home, demanding to know why Pierce, unlike most Concord residents, was not displaying the American flag in honor of the fallen president. "If your hearts are oppressed by events more calculated to awaken profound sorrow and regret than any which have hitherto occurred in our history, mine mingles its deepest regrets and sorrows with yours," Pierce told them. He also adamantly refused to acknowledge that his failure to fly the flag indicated a lack of patriotism. His father had fought in the Revolution and his brothers in the War of 1812, he declared, and he himself had followed that flag into Mexico. "If the period during which I have served our State and country in various situations, commencing more than thirty-five years ago, have left the question of my devotion to the flag, the Constitution, and the Union in doubt, it is too late now to remove it." Having listened raptly to what Pierce said, the crowd gave him three cheers and dispersed.

In late 1865 Pierce became so sick that Sophia Hawthorne dispatched her teenage son Julian to Concord to aid him. Julian described Pierce as quite weak, but he gradually recovered, and in the next two years two projects consumed Pierce's attention. He purchased an eighty-acre shoreline plot in North Hampton, New Hampshire, and had a two-story cottage constructed right at the water's edge, a few miles south of the grand hotel at Rye Beach where he and Jane had often summered prior to his presidency. He also started to clear the remaining land with the intention of farming it. Indeed, soon after his purchase, Pierce personally began plowing the acres that did not need clearing, and in his final years he often referred to himself as an "old farmer."

. . .

For the remainder of his life Pierce spent much of his time shuffling between the rented house in Concord and the cottage at the shore where he spent the late summer and fall. At the cottage he frequently hosted friends such as Clarence March, his nephews, and his nieces. He had, after all, specified the construction of the two-story cottage precisely so that he could have overnight guests. On one occasion, Julian Hawthorne stayed for several weeks. One day the two of them swam nude in the cold surf, and young Hawthorne wrote home with an awed physical description of Pierce, who had then passed sixty years of age: broad chest, slim waist, and heavily muscled arms and legs. All that outdoor labor and sporting activity that Pierce so loved had molded a remarkably fit and powerful physique even in his final years. But much drinking also occurred at the seaside retreat, with wine, brandy, and champagne the preferred potables. It seems likely that Pierce drank heavily even when he was alone since ailments caused by liver failure would ultimately kill him.

Although Pierce repeatedly spurned urgings to run again for president, politics remained in his blood. He closely followed events in the nation's capital after the war. He instinctively sided with Andrew Johnson, whom he lauded in a private letter to the new president, in his battle with congressional Republicans. Johnson, an old Jacksonian Democrat like Pierce, expounded in his various and futile veto messages on the states' rights and strict construction principles so dear to Pierce. When congressional Republicans impeached Johnson in 1868, Pierce was outraged. He greeted the Senate's failure to convict Johnson on the House's jerry-rigged charges with relief. In the late summer of 1868, indeed, Pierce hosted at his cottage James W. Grimes, one of the Republican senators who had voted against Johnson's conviction, and his wife.

Pierce also watched the 1868 Democratic national convention and subsequent election with intent interest. He thought the Democrats had fielded a strong field of potential nominees, and he was pleased with the ascendance of former New York governor Horatio Seymour. Nor, though a loyal Democrat until his last days, was Pierce unhappy with the election of the Republican Ulysses S. Grant that year. It is not clear that Pierce knew that the radical wing of the Republican Party opposed Grant's nomination in 1868. But Grant's campaign slogan, taken from his letter accepting the Republican nomination, was "Let Us Have Peace." Pierce hoped that he might bring about a genuine sectional reconciliation that had eluded Johnson.

Still, the political issue that most engaged Pierce after the Civil War was not partisan. Rather it was the fate of his great friend, former cabinet member, and ex-president of the Confederate States of America, Jefferson Davis. After his capture in May 1865 by Union troops, Davis had been consigned to Fortress Monroe at Old Point Comfort on the southern tip of Virginia's Eastern Shore. Some Republicans demanded that Davis be immediately hanged for treason, but throughout the

remainder of 1865 and all of 1866 the government was content to keep him imprisoned. Finally, the government decided
to prosecute him for treason in a trial to be held in the federal
district court in Richmond, Virginia, and scheduled to start on
May 13, 1867. Perhaps hoping to aid Davis's legal team in that
trial, Pierce determined to visit his old friend. Traveling by
train to Baltimore and then by ship to Old Point Comfort, he
arrived on May 8 with a satchel that may have contained a legal
brief. Because he had failed to notify the military authorities in
advance about his trip, however, he was not permitted to see
Davis until the following day. In a long conversation that lasted
well into the evening, Davis made it clear that he did not need
Pierce's legal help at the trial. His defense team, headed by
Charles O'Conor, one of the leaders of the New York bar,
sufficed. Still, Davis was deeply touched by Pierce's effort.
Before Pierce left, Davis jotted a brief note of thanks: "Given
this day made bright by a visit of my beloved friend and ever
honored chief."

Finally released from military prison, Davis was taken under
guard to Richmond for the civil trial due to start on May 13.
When federal prosecutors declined to start the trial, the federal judge released Davis on $100,000 bail, money put up by a
number of northerners, including Horace Greeley, the editor of
the nation's leading Republican newspaper, the *New York Tribune*. Davis never faced trial in Richmond, perhaps because
federal prosecutors feared they could never get a conviction on
a charge of treason from a jury composed of local citizens. In
any event, Pierce had returned to Concord by the time Davis
was released on bail, and he immediately wrote Davis's wife,
Varina, offering to let them stay in his seaside cottage for as
long as they wanted. During his years in the White House, the
now-childless Franklin and Jane Pierce had become enchanted

by the Davises' young children, and they had visited them frequently. The Davises declined Pierce's offer; they had sent their young children to Canada for schooling, and now that Jefferson Davis had finally been released from prison, they were eager to join them there.

The exchange of letters between Pierce and Varina Davis in the late spring of 1867 about the use of Pierce's shore cottage was their last communication. He would never see Jefferson Davis again. Instead, during the summer of 1867, Pierce started drinking heavily. By September one of his nephews found him quite ill and alone at the cottage. He reported that fact to Clarence March, who correctly attributed it to Pierce's drinking. Pierce rallied in early 1868, but the same pattern continued through the winter of 1869. In the spring of 1869, he was well enough to travel to Baltimore in May to attend and address a meeting of the Society of Cincinnati, to which his revered father had belonged. By late July 1869, however, what proved to be Pierce's final illness set in. In the fall, visitors to his cottage found him "too weak to leave his bed" and "sadly emaciated."

Pierce returned to Concord in late September, where he told two doctors who examined him, "I am convinced I shall not recover." The equivalent of a modern-day hospice worker was hired to watch him in his rented house. He lost consciousness on October 7, and by the early morning of October 8 he was dead.

A few years earlier, Pierce, for the first time, had formally joined a Protestant church. He had consciously chosen St. Paul's Episcopal Church in Concord because the denomination's ministers, unlike Congregationalists, Presbyterians, Baptists, and Methodists, had refused to denounce slavery from their pulpits. The minister of St. Paul's presided at Pierce's funeral after his body had lain in state at the state capitol on

October 11. He was buried next to Jane and their two sons who had survived infancy.

. . .

In 1856, after Pierce had been denied renomination, the *New York Times* sarcastically hoped that Pierce would write a history of his administration because he could say so much about the ingratitude of his party. Quite unlike his successor, James Buchanan, who spent the days after leaving the White House writing a defense of his own administration, Pierce had no intention of drafting a history himself. Instead, he hoped that his secretary of state, William L. Marcy, might do so, but Marcy died in July 1857 before he could begin work on the project. Nor did any other members of Pierce's cabinet show any interest in taking on such a history, although Caleb Cushing would have been the next obvious choice to do so. No defense of Pierce's administration appeared until his personal secretary, Sidney Webster, published one in the early 1890s, long after Pierce had died.

Until quite recently, no subsequent biographer or historian who assessed the Pierce administration treated it as kindly as did Webster. Even when they admitted the honesty of the administration, which compared so favorably to the corruption that stained Buchanan's tenure, they faulted Pierce for a misbegotten patronage policy and a disastrous decision to endorse the Kansas-Nebraska Act that helped bring on the Civil War. And they usually tended to attribute those mistakes to Pierce's alleged character flaws: a weak will, too great of an eagerness to please others, decided prosouthern proclivities. As a result, Pierce has languished near the bottom when historians periodically go about ranking American presidents.

My purpose in this intentionally brief life of Pierce has not been to challenge such rankings or to defend Pierce's administration. Rather it has been to try to explain why Pierce did what he did. And rather than see personal weakness as the source of his missteps in the White House, I attribute Pierce's most fateful political decisions to his obsession with preserving the unity of the Democratic Party.

Milestones

November 23, 1804 — Born in Hillsborough, New Hampshire, son of Anna Kendrick Pierce and Benjamin Pierce

September 1820–August 1824 — Student at Bowdoin College

November 1824 — Presidential election ultimately decided by the U.S. House of Representatives that chose John Quincy Adams, a decision that infuriated Pierce

September 1827 — Admitted to the New Hampshire bar

March 1828 — Elected as moderator of the Hillsborough town meeting, the first of six consecutive elections to that post

November 1828 — Andrew Jackson defeats John Quincy Adams in the presidential election

March 1829	Elected to the first of four terms in the New Hampshire state house of representatives
March 1833–March 1837	Serves two terms in the U.S. House of Representatives
November 19, 1834	Marries Jane Means Appleton of Amherst, New Hampshire
March 1837–February 1842	Serves as U.S. senator for New Hampshire
February 24, 1838	Graves-Cilley duel takes place
November 1844	James K. Polk elected president
January 1845	Secures ouster of John P. Hale from Democratic congressional ticket
May 1846–March 1848	Mexican-American War
August 1846	Wilmot Proviso introduced into Congress
June–December 1847	Serves in Mexico as a brigadier general under the command of Winfield Scott, who will be Pierce's primary opponent in the presidential election of 1852
November 1848	Election of the Whig Zachary Taylor as president

August–September 1850	Passage of the Compromise of 1850
December 1850	Arranges ouster of John Atwood from the Democratic state ticket
November 1850–January 1851	Serves as president of convention to revise New Hampshire's state constitution
June 1852	Receives Democratic nomination for president on the forty-ninth ballot of voting
November 2, 1852	Wins presidential election by a landslide, carrying twenty-seven of thirty-one states
January 1853	Remaining son Benjamin ("Benny") killed in a tragic train accident
March 4, 1853	Takes oath of office as the fourteenth president of the United States
June 1853	Signs a treaty with Mexico for the acquisition of the Gadsden Purchase
January 1854	Buys into the concept of the Nebraska bill during a meeting at the White House
February 1854	U.S. merchant ship *Black Warrior* seized in Havana

May 30, 1854	Signs the Kansas-Nebraska Act into law
September 1854–April 1855	Democrats routed in the North's congressional and gubernatorial elections
October 1854	Ostend Manifesto signed by U.S. foreign ministers James Buchanan, John Y. Mason, and Pierre Soulé
March 1855	Election of the first Kansas territorial legislature with votes cast by Missouri "Border Ruffians"
July 1855	Proslavery laws passed in Kansas
January 1856	Rival "free state" government elections held in Kansas, which Pierce calls "illegal" and "revolutionary"
February 1856	First meetings are held to form national Republican Party
May 1856	"Sack of Lawrence" and Pottawatomie Creek massacre occur
June 1856	Bid for renomination as Democratic presidential candidate defeated at the party's national convention

November 1856	Buchanan elected president with only 45 percent of the popular vote and barely two-fifths of the popular vote in the North, where Republicans carry eleven of sixteen states
March 1857	Leaves White House and Washington, D.C.
December 1857–August 1859	Takes extended sojourn in Madeira and travels throughout Europe
April 1861–April 1865	Civil War, during which Pierce's patriotism is questioned on several occasions
December 2, 1863	Death of Jane Appleton Pierce at age fifty-seven
May 1864	Nathaniel Hawthorne, Pierce's great friend, dies, with Pierce in the next room
October 8, 1869	Dies in Concord, New Hampshire

Selected Bibliography

With two exceptions, I have confined this short bibliography to books and articles I consulted when writing this brief biography and those that I know from previous readings are germane to different aspects of Pierce's life and political career. The exceptions, which I have not read, are Nathaniel Hawthorne's campaign biography of Pierce and Sidney Webster's 1892 history of his administration. I have not listed here the issues of the *New York Times*, *New York Herald*, *Boston Atlas*, and other newspapers that I cite in the text, but Pierce's inaugural address and various messages to Congress while president can be found in the volume *Messages and Papers of the Presidents*, listed below. My book relies heavily on the two modern biographies of Pierce by Roy Franklin Nichols and especially Peter A. Wallner as well as a study of Pierce's presidential administration by Larry Gara. Wallner's two-volume and highly favorable portrait of Pierce is by far the fullest and most thoroughly researched biography of Pierce ever written. I have relied more heavily on these volumes than on any other source in preparing this biography. For New Hampshire politics I have also drawn on the three studies listed below by Donald B. Cole, Lex Renda, and Richard H. Sewell. For the 1850s I have relied on my own research and previous publications as well as other studies of that decade. A microfilm edition of some of Franklin Pierce's Papers is available from the Library of Congress. Finally, the edition of Benjamin Brown French's journal, edited by Donald B. Cole and John J. McDonough, which I list below, contains many illuminating insights about Pierce.

Anbinder, Tyler. *Nativism and Slavery: The Northern Know Nothings and the Politics of the 1850s.* New York: Oxford University Press, 1992.

Cole, Donald B. *Jacksonian Democracy in New Hampshire.* Cambridge: Harvard University Press, 1970.

Cole, Donald B., and John J. McDonough, eds. *Witness to the Young Republic: A Yankee's Journal, 1828–1870, Benjamin Brown French.* Hanover, N.H.: University Press of New England, 1989.

Cooper, William J., Jr. *Jefferson Davis: American.* New York: Alfred A. Knopf, 2000.

Eliot, Charles Winslow. *Winfield Scott: The Soldier and the Man.* New York: Macmillan, 1937.

Freehling, William W. *The Road to Disunion.* Vol. 1, *Secessionists at Bay, 1776–1854.* New York: Oxford University Press, 1990.

———. *The Road to Disunion.* Vol. 2, *Secessionists Triumphant, 1854–1861.* New York: Oxford University Press, 2007.

Gara, Larry. *The Presidency of Franklin Pierce.* Lawrence: University Press of Kansas, 1991.

Gienapp, William E. *The Origins of the Republican Party, 1852–1856.* New York: Oxford University Press, 1987.

Hawthorne, Nathaniel. *The Life of Franklin Pierce.* Boston: Ticknor, Reed, and Fields, 1852.

Holt, Michael F. "The Democratic Party, 1828–1860." In *History of U.S. Political Parties*, vol. 1, ed. Arthur M. Schlesinger, Jr. New York: Chelsea House and R. W. Bowker, 1973.

————. *The Fate of Their Country: Politicians, Slavery Extension, and the Coming of the Civil War.* New York: Hill and Wang, 2004.

————. *The Political Crisis of the 1850s.* New York: W. W. Norton, 1981.

————. "The Politics of Impatience: The Origins of Know Nothingism." *Journal of American History* 60 (1973), 309–31.

————. *The Rise and Fall of the American Whig Party: Jacksonian Politics and the Onset of the Civil War.* New York: Oxford University Press, 1999.

Johannsen, Robert W. *Stephen A. Douglas.* New York: Oxford University Press, 1973.

————. *To the Halls of the Montezumas: The Mexican War in American Imagination.* New York: Oxford University Press, 1985.

Nevins, Allan. *The Ordeal of the Union: A House Dividing, 1852–1857.* New York: Charles Scribner's Sons, 1947.

Nichols, Roy Franklin. *Disruption of American Democracy.* New York: Macmillan, 1948.

————. *Franklin Pierce: Young Hickory of the Granite Hills.* Philadelphia: University of Pennsylvania Press, 1931, completely revised edition 1958.

————. "The Kansas-Nebraska Act: A Century of Historiography." *Mississippi Valley Historical Review* 43 (1956), 187–212.

Potter, David M. *The Impending Crisis, 1848–1861.* Edited and completed by Don E. Fehrenbacher. New York: Harper and Row, 1976.

Renda, Lex. *Running on the Record: Civil War–Era Politics in New Hampshire.* Charlottesville: University Press of Virginia, 1997.

Richardson, James D., ed. *Messages and Papers of the Presidents, 1789–1897.* Vol. 5. Washington, D.C.: Government Printing Office, 1897.

Sewell, Richard H. *John P. Hale and the Politics of Abolition.* Cambridge: Harvard University Press, 1965.

Wallace, Michael. "Changing Concepts of Party in the United States." *American Historical Review* 74 (1968), 453–91.

Wallner, Peter A. *Franklin Pierce: Martyr for the Union.* Concord, N.H.: Plaidswede, 2007.

———. *Franklin Pierce: New Hampshire's Favorite Son.* Concord, N.H.: Plaidswede, 2004.

Webster, Sidney. *Franklin Pierce and His Administration.* New York: D. Appleton, 1892.

Index

northern Democrats (*cont'd*)
elections of 1856 and, 114
Kansas-Nebraska and divisions in,
76–78, 82–83, 85–86
Pierce and split in, 67–68
Pierce nomination in 1852 and,
41, 43
Pierce renomination battle of 1856
and, 97–98, 102
Wilmot Proviso and, 32
northern Know Nothings
Kansas-Nebraska and merger of,
with Republicans, 92, 99–101
rise of, 86–90
northern Whigs, 31–32
Compromise of 1850 and, 35–36,
38–39
elections of 1852 and, 36–37,
43–45
elections of 1852–55 and weakness
of, 47–48, 84–86, 88–89
Kansas-Nebraska and, 80, 82–83

O'Conor, Charles, 130
Ohio, 83–84, 88–89, 104, 110
Ohio Peace Democrats, 124
Opposition Party, 85, 89
Order of the Star Spangled Banner,
87
Order of United Americans, 87–88
Oregon territory, 72
Ostend Manifesto (1854), 64, 65

Panic
of 1837, 20
of 1857, 119
paper money, 11–12, 20
patronage, 66–70, 79, 95, 101–2,
121, 132
Peace Convention of 1861, 123
Pennsylvania, 13, 41, 51, 57, 67, 70,
83, 89, 97, 104, 109
People's Party, 85
petition, right of, 18, 20
Phillips, Philip, 76–77
Pierce, Anna Kendrick (mother), 5
Pierce, Benjamin (father), 5–6, 9–10,
28
Pierce, Benjamin (son), 33
death of, 50
Pierce, Franklin
abolitionist petitions and Gag Rule
and, 17–21

annual message to Congress of
1853, 71–72, 79
annual message to Congress of
1855, 58
annual message to Congress of
1856 and attack on antislavery
forces, 110–14
appointed U.S. attorney for New
Hampshire by Polk, 27
birth, education, and youth of, 3,
5–9
birth and death of first child and,
18
birth of son Frank Robert and, 21
Buchanan presidency and,
115–16
burned in effigy in New
Hampshire, 102
cabinet selections of, and focus on
party unity, 47–52
Catholic vote and, 87
Civil War and, 2, 119–20,
122–25
Clayton-Bulwer treaty and,
57–59
Compromise of 1850 and, 36,
40–41, 65
Crimean War and, 58–59
Cuba and, 59–65
death of, 127–28, 131–32
death of Hawthorne and,
126–27
death of Lincoln and, 127
death of Marcy, Dobbin, and
Means and, 117
death of sons and, 1–2, 18, 50
death of wife and, 125–27
Democratic unity as obsession of,
2–4, 22–23, 25–26, 47–48,
65–71, 84, 121–22, 133
diplomatic appointments of, as
president, 54–65, 68
domestic policy and, 71
doughface label and, 19, 44
drinking of, 7–8, 23, 29, 125, 127,
128, 131
early political ascent of, in New
Hampshire, 1, 9–11, 24–25
elected to U.S. House, 1, 7, 13–15,
17–19, 27
elected to U.S. Senate, 1, 19–22
election of, as president, in 1852,
1, 7, 25–26, 34, 39–46

ABOUT THE AUTHOR

MICHAEL F. HOLT is the Langbourne M. Williams Professor of American History at the University of Virginia. He is the author of six books, including the award-winning *The Rise and Fall of the American Whig Party* and *By One Vote: The Disputed Presidential Election of 1876*. He lives in Charlottesville, Virginia.